TWAYNE'S WORLD AUTHORS SERIES

A Survey of the World's Literature

Sylvia E. Bowman, Indiana University
GENERAL EDITOR

FRANCE

Maxwell A. Smith, Guerry Professor of French, Emeritus
The University of Chattanooga
Former Visiting Professor in Modern Languages
The Florida State University

EDITOR

Guy de Maupassant

(TWAS 265)

TWAYNE'S WORLD AUTHORS SERIES (TWAS)

The purpose of TWAS is to survey the major writers
—novelists, dramatists, historians, poets, philosophers,
and critics—of the nations of the world. Among the
national literatures covered are those of Australia,
Canada, China, Eastern Europe, France, Germany,
Greece, India, Italy, Japan, Latin America, the Nether-
lands, New Zealand, Poland, Russia, Scandinavia, Spain,
and the African nations, as well as Hebrew, Yiddish,
and Latin Classical literatures. This survey is comple-
mented by Twayne's United States Authors Series
and English Authors Series.

The intent of each volume in these series is to present a
critical-analytical study of the works of the writer; to
include biographical and historical material that may be
necessary for understanding, appreciation, and critical
appraisal of the writer; and to present all material in
clear, concise English—but not to vitiate the scholarly
content of the work by doing so.

Guy de Maupassant

By A. H. WALLACE

University of Tennessee-Knoxville

ABOUT THE AUTHOR

Professor Albert H. Wallace is currently the coordinator for graduate studies in French at the University of Tennessee. He holds degrees from Presbyterian College and the Universities of Alabama and North Carolina. His specialties are nineteenth-century French Literature and Comparative Literature.

Twayne Publishers, Inc.   ::   New York

Preface

MAUPASSANT believed firmly that criticism's only valid concern was with how well the writer had achieved what he had set out to do. He did not like the critic who insisted upon questioning the morality of the work, the taste of the artist, or the worthiness of the quest.

The baffling quantity and inconsistent quality of Maupassant's literary output make for stormy and inconclusive debating between those on the one hand who wish to deny his greatness and those on the other who wish to remove what doubts exist concerning it. There is so much, that one is encouraged to enter into idle speculating and theorizing on what the grand plan was and almost to ignore what has been achieved. This study will concern itself with what Maupassant has done and how his achievement was both the result and revelation of his life. If Maupassant saw all the strange pieces as parts of a grand scheme, he left no detailed outline of it for us. A study of his life yields evidence of its intricate relationship to his work and suggests that he was much more than an objective observer and recorder of the world in which he lived. His choice of subject matter and his manner of reflecting it are both consistent with causes he championed passionately. The time was right for him: seldom did he have to be so obvious as to discredit his claim at objectivity. But the consistency with which he occupied himself with certain pieces of the puzzle does hint at a plan whose limits and prejudices are strongly personal.

Many critics still downgrade Maupassant's works, condescending to admire masterpieces such as *Boule de Suif* and *Pierre et Jean,* but parsimonious with their praise, often using the great size of his work against him. The time is appropriate for a pinpointing of the achievements obscured by this vast and confusing size. Readers and even critics have been too willing to accept the prejudiced and often invalid judgment of the few who have thoroughly read all of Maupassant. Their trust, perhaps, stems from a reluctance to read a vast outpouring, often termed as that of just another nineteenth-century Realist-Naturalist, and not from any honest conviction that eleven Maupassant stories and *Pierre et Jean* encompass all that is laudable about his work. That Maupassant did not enlist readers by implying that there was some ultimate dream to be shared with the few willing to pursue his thread of thought through the vast labyrinth of his writings may result from his admiration for Flaubert who never suggested any final revelation as the reward for reading his entire output. Like his "tutor-father," Maupassant was too impatient with himself to maintain the steady course that writers more sure of their *Weltanschauung* and of their limitations are wont to do. He was always a young writer, with all the faults and glories appertaining thereunto. But it appears true that his scorn for plans, for critics, for pedantry, for pontificating, and for coining some grandiose, all-embracing title for his work has cost him critical readers and has contributed to the opinion that he is strictly second rate.

He was interested in fame and fortune. Perhaps that is why he made no systematic compilation of his esthetic opinions. Maupassant was a man in a hurry who regarded creating as the best way to get "there." He was a doer, not a commentator. But his work speaks for him.

All of the passages cited or quoted are from the Conard edition. The translations are my own.

Acknowledgments

I wish to thank Professor Maxwell Smith for offering me the opportunity to do this work. His patience and confidence are also sincerely appreciated.

A great teacher, Professor Alfred G. Engstrom, is due more thanks than I can express for the enthusiasm for the nineteenth century which he instilled in me.

A very special note of thanks to my wife, Nancy, who has been and is my inspiration.

Contents

Chronology

1850   August 5, birth of Henry-René-Albert Guy de Maupassant.

1854   Maupassant family moved to the château of Granville-Ymauville, near Le Havre.

1856   Birth of Maupassant's brother, Hervé.

1859   Student at Lycée Napoléon, Paris.

1860

1861   Sojourn in Etretat.

1862

1864   Student at the ecclesiastic school of Yvetot.

1864   Met Swinburne.

1868   Took up studies at Lycée de Rouen.

1869   Bachelier ès lettres. Student of Law at Paris.

1872   Position in Ministry of the Marine.

1874   Meeting with Zola at Flaubert's apartment. First writing published in obscure journal.

1875   Struggles to write dramas.

1876   The Médan group formed.

1878   From Ministry of the Marine to the Ministry of Public Instruction.

1880   Publication of *Boule de Suif*. Cuts himself free from a career in the ministries and dedicates himself entirely to writing.

1880   Journey to Corsica. Beginning of wanderlust.

1881   Trip to Algeria.

1883   *Une Vie* published.

1885   Success of *Bel-Ami*.

1887   Declining success with the novel noted with publication of *Mont-Oriol*. A second trip to Algeria.

1888   *Pierre et Jean*.

1889   Very poor novel, *Fort comme la Mort*.

1890   Sojourn in England.

1891   Series of treatments for the "malady."

1892   Suicide attempt. Internment at Dr. Blanche's sanatorium.

1893   Death and burial in Montparnasse cemetery.

CHAPTER 1

The Shadowy Figure—What Can Be Seen
from Without His Work

I The Biographical Problem and Laure de Maupassant

MAUPASSANT'S mother protected him from the womb to the grave and his reputation beyond. It is unfortunate for criticism that Laure de Maupassant was so solicitous of her son's reputation, for in censoring what *she* considered damaging to *her* view of what his image was, she left us with considerable information about her own natural prudery and possessiveness but little of value about the one in whom we are most interested. Her censorship has moreover necessitated one to rely almost entirely upon his works as a source for an intimate understanding of Maupassant as a person. And though knowing little about an author as a person can be a blessing, in the case of Maupassant it has often led to misconceptions and uncalled-for psychological criticisms of his work. Many of his interpreters have found it impossible to avoid sponsoring their own personal theses to the detriment of sound criticisms.

As if she were fated to be the mother of Flaubert's most ardent admirer and disciple, Laure de Maupassant grew up with her son's future idol. Her brother, Alfred le Poittevin, was Flaubert's literary tutor-confessor. The former brought Shakespeare into the Maupassant household along with his admiring young cohort. Poittevin was the kind of intellectual who had a peculiar attraction for men of real creative genius: he talked brilliantly but wrote with more intellectual brilliance than creative imagination. Laure, however, regarded him as a complete genius. And when it became evident that her firstborn resembled the sainted brother strikingly, she decided at once that her son was destined to literary greatness. Her only doubt was ever about how much time he would be given to create, for Alfred's premature death cast an ominous shadow across her dreams for Guy.

II *Gustave de Maupassant*

Laure raised him by the sea, at Etretat, glorying every day in his resemblance to Alfred le Poittevin. She seems to have shut out her husband from the beginning. He had been a biological necessity, but now he counted for little. Nevertheless, the insidious presence of Gustave de Maupassant made itself felt: Guy early showed himself more inclined to idleness than to the lonely, cruel work that his mentor, Flaubert, was going to demand of him. He was incapable of experiencing the kind of idealism that motivated Flaubert. Though Maupassant always sided with his diligent mother, there was much in him that suggested that had his father cared to, he could have kept his wife from capturing him for art.

Maupassant's recurring treatment of the cuckold has little of the good humor and rollicking fun that had become traditional in the French treatment of the theme. It is not hard to guess that he knew his father who richly deserved to be cuckolded would have been as asinine a victim as any of his character dupes, and that his austere, humorless treatment of an old theme was occasioned by his wish to punish the man he wished would take command of his life. But he belonged to his mother through the default of a thoughtless, spoiled father whose primary concern seemed to be how to bluff his way through the expensive life his tastes required after he had wasted his inheritance. The father's small concern for his children or wife except as their existence was of some positive profit to himself left no course for Guy but to become a "mama's boy" and occasionally avenge himself against the possessiveness of overzealous mothers in fictional diatribes. If, as so many critics have imagined, there is much of Laure de Maupassant in the figure of Jeanne de Lamare, the heroine of *Une Vie*, it is safe to assume that the complaint of Jeanne's son that he would have none of his mother's planning his life and that he was not made for the sad and deadening shade of her fawning reflects an occasional rebellious mood on Maupassant's part against his own mother. As we shall see, he nourishes a contempt for the generality of womanhood that equals or even surpasses his disdain for weak males, and he leaves us sure that he thought nothing of the human race as a whole, but only admired its rare, unique specimens. Even the extent of his love for his mother is cast into doubt, though critics generally accept the notion that Laure de Maupassant was one woman for whom Guy had no unkind words or thoughts.

The father's willing acceptance of a separation from Laure doomed whatever slim chance there might have been for Maupassant to have any real respect for husbands and fathers. Laure, herself, with her worshipful promotion of the myth of Alfred le Poittevin, contributed to her son's growing conviction that only *single* males deserved one's trust and confidence. Perhaps these early impressions had as much to do with his failure to marry and his building of the myth of cuckoldry as any other single factor. There is a distinct parallel between the manner in which Maupassant dispatches Jeanne's husband, Julien de Lamare in *Une Vie*, and the manner in which Gustave de Maupassant goes out of the life of his son: the fathers were not necessary. Yet, as famous a husband-baiter as is Maupassant, there remains the hint in *Une Vie* that the author wished fathers *were* the kind of people who took charge.

III *Gustave Flaubert*

A strong paternal influence in his life would certainly have affected his attitude toward husbands and fathers. As it turned out, it is fortunate for us and for the son that the father did not excel in the paternal role. Maupassant's quest for a father was an important aspect of his career. It was a short quest that led him to Flaubert who was to suggest to his adopted "son" many of the attitudes and ideas that were the leaven for stories and to give him that special kind of fatherly scolding that every opinionated, brilliant but undisciplined young writer needs. Flaubert's sermonizing on the subject of diligence and self-discipline was just what the doctor ordered; but Maupassant would have accepted the advice from *no one else*. Asceticism was too alien to his nature; but it appears that in trying to warp his life to resemble that of the master, Maupassant discovered that there was much more to be had from work than from rowing and dreaming. Too, he found that Flaubert's observations upon human frailty, on literature, and on how to write touched a sensitive chord in his soul. We shall see that Flaubert's influence upon Maupassant's choice of theme and character suggests an important relationship between the two that is seldom mentioned.

Their similar manner of viewing reality is more interesting than the cold fact that Flaubert served as Maupassant's literary mentor. Perhaps the teacher did not want his pupil to imitate him in anything but his dedication to art as an ideal; but it is nonetheless evident that Maupassant confronts us with characters whose problems and frustrations take the stage in a world which strongly resembles the one Flaubert depicted. The relationship between the two, often depicted by critics as merely the story of a not-so-eager successful author taking under his wing the son of a dear friend as a favor and then discovering a real fondness for his charge, needs to be reexamined in the light of how it affected Maupassant's stories. It appears that this literary relationship had a far more direct influence upon Maupassant's work than has been supposed. There is no reason to believe that the law which allows mediocrity to triumph in the person of Homais in *Madame Bovary*, for instance, is not the same law at work in *Pierre et Jean* where the unimaginative and conforming Jean flashes upward while his sensitive, imaginative nonconformist brother is not allowed to rise. That the Jeans of the world succeed appears every bit as abhorrent to Maupassant as it is to Flaubert that a Homais will invariably triumph. There are, then, valid reasons for seeing Flaubert's influence upon Maupassant as extending into the very fiber of his thought, and we shall look more closely at some of them.

IV *War*

Another major force in determining much of Maupassant's work was the Franco-Prussian War; without it we would not have some of his most thoughtful work, nor would we see Maupassant as one who wore that unique badge of pride emblazoned with the myth of their country's invulnerability that all Frenchmen wear. It took the shocking realization that he was just as foolish and proud as any of his compatriots to draw forth from him some of his finest characters and stories. He tells his stories of defeat and retreat with wit and an eye for the droll. That is why Maupassant comes very close to fingering the pulse of his contemporaries and of Frenchmen of all times. He shows himself emotionally more mature than his fellow countrymen, however, in refusing to haggle over the insoluble questions of war's inevitability or futility; rather he presents us with characters who are alive because they do whatever they do best in order to frustrate tyranny. This quality enlists the sympathy of all who have known or imagined the conqueror's heel.

V *Paris*

Paris stained Maupassant's view of life. The city was for him what it had been for so many of his illustrious predecessors, beginning with Villon. He saw how its denizens came to extravagant or violent acts because there was something about the city that could inspire unrealizable dreams of wealth and influence in very ordinary minds. Perhaps because he realized the foolishness of the mistaken dreams of the young who come to Paris, he clung stubbornly to his interest in physical superiority, canoeing upon the Seine with furious dedication instead of shining in the city's literary salons. The Seine gave him a place to work off the frustrating sequestration of his jobs in Ministries, a place where he could exhibit his provincial vigor which so contrasted with the pale flabbiness of the victims of Paris' hellish industrialization and of its cluttered literary salons. Whenever Flaubert came to Paris, Maupassant would behave like the indulgent son, putting art before rowing and pleasing his "father" by writing little wicked entertainments for him and a privileged few of their friends. And afterward he would return dutifully to his hated desk at the Ministry with a folder filled with pages Flaubert had bluelined, convinced instead of piqued by the master's criticism.

The hard reality of knowing that he was not a Parisian gave Maupassant the kind of insight which allowed him to describe so successfully all of those misfits who came from the provinces to be office clerks in the big city. Few writers have approached Maupassant's understanding of the disillusionment and confusion of the young attracted from their earthy existence by misleading ads only to be consumed, faceless and nameless, in the blast furnace of governmental or corporation agencies. The nothingness of his position as a glorified clerk in Paris contributed much to Maupassant's future as a writer.

The literary salons, though generally repugnant to Maupassant, implemented his career as an artist. Had it not been for Paris he would not have made the acquaintance of Turgenev, who became his best foreign literary agent, and who, as we shall see, doubtless served as a lasting literary model. Flaubert knew that seasonally, Paris had the world's greatest writers, composers, and artists. Hence he kept an apartment in Paris where Maupassant was able to meet Paul Alexis and be drawn into the group who later wrote their stories under the title, *Soirées de Médan*. Flaubert, then, was instrumental in the publication of *Boule de Suif* which, because of its success, made Maupassant no longer dependent upon the salary he earned at the Ministry of the Marine. His freedom he used to good advantage. And the *conte*, he realized, was to be his forte. Happily, he turned his efforts from lyric and narrative poetry to favor what he now knew he did well.

He soon learned about unscrupulous publishers who would abuse their contributors where a profit was to be made. The editor of the journal in which Maupassant published his poetry, seeing the possibility of a fast "buck," brought out an unexpurgated version of the poems: when the authorities became incensed because they deemed the poetry to appeal only to prurient sensibilities, the editor not only left Maupassant holding the bag but helped the authorities against him! Even Flaubert's sympathy because of his recent experience with *Madame Bovary* did not console Maupassant. And though he cajoled his own publisher, Charpentier, into publishing a volume of Maupassant's poetry, the latter did not return to lyric poetry as a primary vocation.

VI   *"Making It" as a Writer*

Now Maupassant was firmly committed to the *conte* and *nouvelle* as the forms which represented his best chance of success. Doubtless, Flaubert's enthusiasm for the story, *Boule de Suif*, went further than public approbation in convincing Maupassant that he had chosen wisely. Like so many writers, he had once harbored the hope of being a dramatist. And though he did not have even a middling success in the genre, the discipline imposed upon him by dramatic form had its beneficial results. He learned to write dialogue with the bulletlike directness of the fine dramatist, and some of the plays he had written were later transformed into fine short stories.

He must have sensed immediately the truly outstanding quality of *Boule de Suif* to be its character delineation. For the mark of his greatness became his ability to turn external observations of his neighbors into the proper indices to what made them tick. It is amazing to see how well Maupassant uses the external detail to direct the reader into his characters' minds. They appear simple because he has studied their external behavior patterns so thoroughly and chosen so well the *revelatory detail* that we are fooled into believing we have known them. Let us not overlook the fact, however, that Maupassant's characters are complicated in a human way, that is to say, they convince us that they are bumpkins or simpletons through their creator's ability to convince us they are what they are, members of our own complicated race.

Maupassant's ambition to become a first-rate novelist doubtless stems from his admiration for Flaubert and from the belief that there was both money and glory awaiting the successful novelist. Unfortunately, he never realized how peculiarly suited his talent was to the short story and how ill-suited were his powers of observation to the novel. *Pierre et Jean* was a popular and critical success and merits the continuing attention of serious scholars of literature. But Maupassant seemed to believe there was strength in length and kept attempting to write a longer and longer novel. The longer they became the less they reflected their author's unique talent, which was to summarize a situation or a character in the briefest possible terms. The long lyric passages and the heavy-handed philosophical pronouncements of most of the novels leave the admirer of Maupassant dismayed and the casual reader with an unread book in his library. Sociologists, psychologists, and screen writers have contributed to the success of *Bel-Ami*. It certainly cannot compare favorably with Marivaux's *Le Paysan parvenu*, though it is cut from the same forest. All of his novels contain their "remarkable" passages—*Mont-Oriol, Notre Coeur*, and others—but these pages are strange oases in vast deserts. The serious reader will almost at once "lock-on" to the drama and message of *Pierre et Jean* because we are all used to situations which consist of the once-in-a lifetime event that changes the whole course of a family's destiny. But there is no such center of interest in the other novels of Maupassant. So many of them appear simply to be the flotsam of his novelistic aspirations circling aimlessly the nucleus of his literary achievement as a short-story writer. Tolstoy praised *Une Vie*. The informed reader can guess why.

Maupassant does not remain as impersonal as so many critics

have suggested. In his novels, in particular, he grows boring with his narrow-mindedness. The extremely personal nature of some of the material in his novels, for example, in *Une Vie* and *Pierre et Jean*, demonstrates how he used situations in his life to the point of being autobiographical. The novels, in particular, show that Maupassant was far from the detached, emotionally remote observer that was supposed to describe the Naturalist and which many see as describing Maupassant. The strain of autobiography in his work, I feel, is evident, and is an important facet of his art which has but hastily, if at all, been plumbed.

Maupassant was invested with the parsimony and acquisitiveness of his Norman counterparts. Nearing the end of his life, his interest in money led him to a number of unwise decisions concerning his literary output. His publisher, Havard, whether unwittingly or not, convinced him to make a fool of himself by defending mediocre novels as masterpieces. It appears to the casually informed acquaintance of Maupassant that he let himself suppose inferior works were great, measuring their quality in terms of the money he was making from them. But he was too good a judge of literature to be fooled, even by his own outpourings, except when he was suffering from a seizure. We must conclude that on occasions his desire for fame and profit overwhelmed his better judgment. After all, the question of money is one of his major themes because he too was a clerk on a low salary who saw that just existing could consume every penny a man could muster. And Maupassant had no inclination for the bland life. He, like his mother, felt himself an aristocrat and entitled to expensive tastes: "La Guillette," the lovely retreat he bought after becoming a success, was furnished in a manner that left nothing to be desired.

Travel was a big part of his life. He considered it the privilege of the artist. Much of the money he earned from his successes was squandered in regions that later were to inspire some of his most interesting works. At least he was able to tell himself that the "investment" had paid dividends. Indeed, his work would seem singularly vapid without his intense interest in the behavior of the peoples outside his beloved France. We would begin to wonder if he weren't merely another artist capable of creating the stereotype of a region, without a glimmering of how the provincials he created were a universal replica.

Literary fame encouraged Maupassant to be himself, vehemently. Why be a poseur? He could afford even to make a fetish of avoiding the kind of company first-rate writers often find themselves in. No salons for him unless *he* approved! It is relatively certain that he would have said something about his *"art poétique"* in his glory days had he been a regular participant in literary societies; and perhaps his ostentatious avoiding of the salons has left us with too many unresolved questions about his literary opinions. But he was a man who stood free of the politics of academic approbation, who had no truck with the mediocrities who professed to love letters so long and loud that they failed to produce any, and who had only scorn for the academic chairs from which medium talents pronounced their literary "Bulls." It has cost us something not to have Maupassant's critical opinions, but one wonders if they would not have been a jumble of prejudices better left unsaid. He never began to talk directly about his writings and theories until the deterioration of his mental capacities had become so acute as to cloud his remarks with suspicion or totally void them. And the criticism he wrote for pay is highly suspect. But there are, in works that do not purport to deal with criticism, some very interesting and imaginative critical insights which we shall explore.

VII *The Disease*

His disease was a curious one. As early as his relationship with Flaubert, he complained of nervous seizures. And Flaubert, always the disciplined artist, suggested to Maupassant that moderation in his activities and dedication to writing were the best cure. But Maupassant was a rebel. And he suspected "his father" of denying him the privilege of experiencing the fullness of life. So, despite Flaubert's insistence that writers had to deny themselves the kind of life others lived, Maupassant obeyed the call of his senses, an unfortunate obeisance which only aggravated his already blurred vision, and magnified his bouts with hallucination. To relieve the terrible migraines of syphilis, he tried ether, cocaine, morphine, or hashish. At first, of course, there was temporary relief; but ultimately he suffered *more* because of his use of the drugs, and his mental problems mounted alarmingly. He did not, however, become addicted.

Maupassant did not accomplish his masterpieces while under the influence of a drug. The chilling insights into madness so prevalent in his work were obtained through intensive and cruel self-analysis. His extraordinary retentive powers did allow him to present us with some of the most startlingly accurate accounts to be found in literature of the dreams and aberrations of a madman, heightening his madness by trying to relieve it with drugs. When he overindulged in ether inhaling, the writing he was doing evidenced a strong dependence upon the olfactory sense. His inclination toward morbidity would be increased alarmingly by the odors of his medications. The more severe his disease, the more necessary isolation became to him and, paradoxically, the more extensive were his fears of being alone. He tormented himself with loneliness, however, perhaps in a mood of self-flagellation for not having followed the teachings of his "father" during his younger days.

Maupassant's self-imposed solitude led to fear and provided him with an uncanny insight into the terror that loneliness can multiply even in the most sound of the race. This comprehension of terror is what gives to his fantastic stories their extraordinarily credible quality. The stories, *Lui?*, *Le Horla*, and *Qui Sait?* are among his most widely read and appreciated. The autobiographic character of these stories leaves us with a fairly extensive image of what Maupassant suffered, and hence they will be studied in detail in the appropriate place.

There is little doubt that hallucination so subverted Maupassant's capacity for drawing rational conclusions in the latter part of his illness that he finally became incapable of distinguishing between his wildest fancies and reality. The last years were sad. His erratic behavior caused those who were jealous or for one reason or another wished him ill to broadcast and exaggerate his case. They were sad years because they were wasted ones: his better days were used up in fruitless searchings for a cure in medical books, in experimenting with quack remedies, and in generally feeding his hypochondria. These useless things occupied him when he should have been writing. He convinced himself that an illness plaguing Taine was identical to his; and when the latter made a remarkable recovery he took heart, sure that he himself would recover. All of it was madness: he saw what he wanted to see, and his enemies were quick to mock him for it.

VIII   *The End*

Neither friends nor physicians would tell him the truth about his illness. They were perhaps trying to be kind, to prevent his despairing. Their efforts were to no avail. His beloved valet, François Tassart, despite the close watch he kept on him and upon available instruments of self-destruction, found him with his throat slit, the straight-razor still in his hand. One wonders how fortunate it really was that he found him in time to save his life for more torment and then a straitjacket. Fate had spared him so that Edmond de Goncourt could top all of his other disparaging descriptions of him with one of a madman in his cell. The public gorged itself cruelly upon such pieces, reveling in the fall of a titan.

Maupassant achieved a great deal in the realm of art. He made a large imprint upon the politics and society of his time without inspiring a revolution or even directly being the author of a reform. What he did was to examine the platitudes by which his fellow countrymen lived in such a way as to cause others to reconsider them. In time what he had to say, his concerns with prejudiced laws and statesmen, were to influence those who came after him. He possessed a rare ability to understand the small, almost unnoticed episodes of human experience, and to so enhance them by his art as to make other men understand both the pettiness and the nobility of all human endeavor.

Maupassant died calmly on July 6, 1893. Zola delivered the graveside eulogy at Montparnasse cemetery.

CHAPTER 2

Cuckoldry in Maupassant's Writing and His Life With Father

I A Message He Did Not Want to Speak

MAUPASSANT is more kind to women than to men in his writings. This is nowhere more evident than in the fact that he wrote so many stories about cuckoldry where the male cuckold is not simply ridiculed, but is presented as pathologically weak and inferior to the female whose antipathy for his inanity drives her to make a cuckold of him. The reader cannot often escape the message: Maupassant thought that an inferior man and his convention-oriented society were justification enough for a woman's cuckolding of her husband and that the weak male victims deserved a writer's contempt, not his sympathy. Yet many are led by anecdote and imprecise statements about Maupassant's "misogyny" to conclude that even stories dealing with cuckoldry were veiled attacks on the female which stemmed from a desire to defend the notion of male superiority. Such a conclusion distorts one's perception of the biographical evidence that appears everywhere in his fiction and further leads to a confusion as to the general meaning and consistency of his vast work.

Maupassant always experienced a personal pang at seeing a man in the process of being duped by his wife, though he loved to write about such a situation. France of the nineteenth century had far more permissive rules for the behavior of women than the English-speaking countries of the same era, but it is evident that Maupassant overestimated the extent of the promiscuity of French married woman. This exaggeration is in direct proportion to his personal hurt as is evidenced by his brooding treatment of cuckoldry. Few of these stories contain that good-humored ribaldry of the tradition of the fabliaux under whose influence he was both intuitively and consciously writing.

It has been suggested that Maupassant is a "mother's boy." But certainly not by choice! If his father had been the kind of domineering genius who coincided with what Maupassant's masculine pride told him a man should be, if the elder Maupassant had verified the he-man qualities and dazzling charm Maupassant ascribed to himself, then perhaps Maupassant's art would not have been so fraught with males who are asinine victims of females whose dominance is due only to their prey's weaknesses. As the hero in *Lui?* says: "I am certain that eight out of ten husbands are cuckolds" (XXVI, 93). Cuckoldry is one of the dominant themes in Maupassant. It begins in the early poem "Sommation" and persists until almost the last story.[1]

II   *The Cuckolder*

An examination of a few stories will demonstrate how an author transmuted his own life into fiction. And though it is dangerous to seek personal experiences as the prime source for the stories of any author, the critic of Maupassant who did not investigate the extent of correlation between his life and stories would be derelict. *Le Testament* depicts a situation which encourages and, in the end, justifies a wife's cuckolding her husband. The wife, married for her money and betrayed from the beginning by her husband, had, herself, taken a lover. And now in her will she confesses, pardons the husband's infidelity which had driven her to adultery, but affirms her right to dispose of her property as she chooses. She chooses to leave her entire estate to her lover who is, in turn, to give it to their bastard son, René, whom the philandering husband had with understandable complacency assumed to be his own. There is here evident a hint of Maupassant's personal misery over having had a father who he supposed cared little for Laure de Maupassant; in the author's eyes, his own father had done all the wrong things and escaped any sort of retribution because of fate's indulgence and his mother's long-suffering and determination to protect the family.

The situation described in *Le Testament* so haunted Maupassant that he used aspects of it in *Une Vie* and later with but minor changes in the celebrated *Pierre et Jean*. The narrator in *Le Testament* expresses Maupassant's admiration for a wife who avenges herself of her husband's infidelity. Might not we suppose that the hero's vehement defense of his mother's adultery—"Very

well, I contend that my mother's will is one of the most beautiful,
the most loyal, the greatest things that a woman could concoct"
(VIII, 165)—to be an expression of Maupassant's admiration for
his mother and anger toward his father?

It is true that all of Maupassant's stories do not attempt to
justify cuckoldry. Remarkable is the fact, however, that Maupassant so persistently presents situations in which the wife's adultery
is defended, even elevated as the act of a superior being; and all
the more remarkable in the repertoire of a man often accused of
misogyny and of being motivated by a secret passion to ridicule
and dominate womankind. Having written stories in which cuckoldry is presented merely as a fact of nineteenth-century life—a
latent possibility of femininity—why does Maupassant return to
the theme already once demonstrated that the husband who is
cuckolded is but getting his just deserts? It must be that he was
never able to resist exploring the possibilities of a situation which
he felt his father's behavior and that of men like him encouraged.
Doubtless, he would have justified his mother had she decided
to behave in the manner of some of his female characters. Maupassant was bitter because his father, like so many husbands, did not
measure up and was, in comparison to his wife, a mediocre,
pusillanimous creature.

The author, on occasion, cared nothing about justifying the
adulterous wife. In *Le Vengeur* he tells of a man who married his
friend's widow. The deceased had obviously been too old to
satisfy the flaming passions of his young wife. This the widow's
husband realizes, and the realization haunts him with doubts
about her fidelity, past and present. At length he wheedles from
her a confession that she had taken a lover in her previous marriage. The revelation drives him into a rage during which he beats
her. Afterward, shame and self-justification mingled: "And turning toward her, he approached, ashamed now of having beat her,
but experiencing in the depth of his heart a hatred for that woman who had betrayed the other . . ." (XVI, 181). Here Maupassant
is fascinated with the psychology of a man who almost willfully
allows suspicion to destroy his happiness—not with justifying the
adultery of the wife. The hero proves incapable of generosity toward a woman who shredded convention without what might be
considered due provocation. Maupassant, himself, was choosy
about the conditions which inspired him to defend the female. He

was somewhat stuffy where "women's liberation" was concerned. On occasion he subscribed to the male notion that the rules for women were justifiably more strict than those for men.

III   *The Cuckolded*

Nor does Maupassant hesitate to give his pity to the kind of male who is nothing more than an ungrateful poltroon. In fact, he seems to pride himself on it, as if he had something against the aging wife who has cuckolded her husband. The story, *Fini,* and the novel, *Fort comme la Mort,* describe the older lover's efforts to convince himself that he is still the lover he was at twenty. It is the pathos of the middle-aged man trying to be a young swain that Maupassant features; the husband is of little consequence: it is the aging lover who must prove himself who counts. In neither case can the hero in his forties be satisfied with seducing a woman his own age; the only way to prove himself is to become the lover of his former mistress' daughter, who turns out to be his remembered image of the aging mother. In each case his plans do not succeed. But Maupassant has, nevertheless, shown us another disdainful portrait of the cuckolded husband.

In *Mont-Oriol* Maupassant justifies a wife who cuckolds her husband because he is more interested in money than in her love. But here what one sees more clearly expressed is anti-Semitism: the author delights in portraying the selfish, prototypal Jew as a cuckold. It is a little strange to see a man who wrote a moving story against those who make outsiders of anyone who flaunts the convention of the unacceptability of interracial marriage (*Boitelle,* 1889) display such obvious racial bias, strange until we remember Maupassant's Norman background and his frenzied personal ambition to become wealthy in the publishing industry. Here, as in other cases, Maupassant's genius earns the forgiveness not given his ordinary countrymen; he was not always above their emotional and narrow conceptions of morality and justice.

In *L'Epreuve* we have the husband depicted as a proud boob who cannot conceive of himself as the victim of cuckoldry: "O.K. As for me, I swear to you that had I been cuckolded I'd have discovered it right away" (XXIV, 143). Male vanity makes him oblivious to a fact of social life. It is just this same insufferably ego-motivated blindness that causes a reader to have no sympathy for M. Roland in *Pierre et Jean* or for Bondel, the hero of the above story. The uniqueness of Maupassant's treatment of the theme in *L'Epreuve* is the manner in which he uses Bondel's scornful, malicious wife as both judge and executioner of her husband for his blindness. Though one cannot discount the influence of Maupassant's perception of the marital problems of his own parents upon those of the characters of his invention, he must not fail to point out the manner in which the author transformed these impressions into fictional situations whose inspiration he perhaps no longer recognized. The scorn and the malice of the woman in *L'Epreuve* are pure invention and are related to his view of woman as a destructress. Though doubtless Maupassant's antagonistic attitude toward Gustave de Maupassant as a result of the latter's behavior as a father and husband had the effect of allaying any sympathy for the cuckolded and arousing instead the author's contempt and condemnation of the deceived, he was often tempted to sympathize with the woman, sometimes even implying that the woman who cuckolds her husband is a superior woman. The superior woman who keeps reappearing in his writings has as her model his mother. There are even some traits of hers evident in the witch of *L'Epreuve* who chides her husband's naïveté at not seeing how easily a wife can cuckold her husband, then smiles malignly as he anguishes over the ever-mounting suspicion that she had made him a cuckold. The same motif as the one perfected in *Pierre et Jean* is used: an old and dear friend whom Bondel himself had introduced to his house had been his wife's lover. The proof is in their reunion years after: "Then she looked, turned red, trembled and drew back a pace . . ." (XXIV, 155). But though the novel and the story are similar insofar as the treatment of the husbands is concerned, there is a distinct difference in the quality of the women portrayed, and this difference in turn shows us a Maupassant who could be as tolerant of women as he was intolerant.

IV *Monsieur Parent and Monsieur Roland*

Monsieur Parent, hero of the story by the same name, is so inept and such a willing receptacle of his wife's abuse as to suggest that Maupassant was more moved to revulsion than to sympathetic understanding by such weak men. He degrades M. Parent by having a servant inform him of how he is being cuckolded. And that a servant is allowed to flagellate him with the news which Pierre's father in *Pierre et Jean* was spared leaves little doubt concerning Maupassant's lack of sentimental pity for Parent. In *Pierre et Jean* Maupassant explores skillfully the interior psychological struggle of those with interesting and sensitive intelligences who find themselves estranged in an unimaginative, convention-ridden world: to be true to themselves they must "sin" and take the consequences of not being understood even by those of equal sensitivity. On the other hand, in this inferior miniature of the novel, Maupassant externalizes, allowing the revelations to be pronounced directly as in a morality play. The father is jolted out of accepting the conventional notion of love and obedience on the part of a wife. *Pierre et Jean* represents a masterful handling of the plot elements in *Monsieur Parent.*

There can be little question in the mind of a sensitive reader as to why the novel is a magnificent artistic achievement while the story is but a mediocre one. The fact that Maupassant was seldom satisfied with one treatment of a situation or theme, though it is often considered a fault, should not be so regarded. As we shall see, though there are repetitions and self-plagiarizations, they show a concern for "getting it right" on the part of the artist. In addition, they help immensely to broaden the critic's understanding of Maupassant's mind and the creative process responsible for his unusual literary fecundity.

Monsieur Parent, deprived of his delusion of spousal fidelity, turns to the instinctive animal fury of the betrayed. He feels sorry for himself, and like Phèdre, masochistically imagines their (his wife's and her lover's) attitude toward him: "How they must have been making fun of him, if he had been duped by them from the very first" (XXI, 34). And the wife in this case is even contemptuous of her lover's admonitions to her not to treat her husband with such disdain as to cause him to revolt. Here, as in *L'Epreuve,* the woman is attacked as a cruel creature—not, however, because Maupassant feels any great sympathy for her victim. Ironically, Limousin, the wife's lover, expresses the only real sympathy for Parent. Left alone, the cuckold decides they are contending that the child is theirs only to torment him, but he cannot bring himself to fight to regain custody of the infant.

Like Maupassant, being alone during the long nights brings him only terror and agonizing appraisals of his troubles. The story's finest lines describe what Maupassant came to know well,

the refreshing quality of the country after years of lonely exile
in the city. Years pass and Parent takes the advice of a friend
to voyage through the countryside for his health. He marvels at
being outside the city of loneliness and is stirred by forgotten reso-
lutions: "all the desires which sleep in the idleness of stagnant
hearts had awakened, moved by this beam of sun on the plains"
(XXI, 62). The story's lack of concentration in straying from the
treatment of cuckoldry to another of those that intrigued its author
most—that of the aging man with his shattered dreams—is typical
of so much of Maupassant's work. It is another flaw that hurts his
literary reputation. But the predilection with this theme provides
an interesting insight into his personal life into which fear of old
age crept prematurely and brought with it a certain deathly confusion to many of his works. Old age for Parent, who had not led
an enlightened and fulfilling life, then, vies with cuckoldry for our
attention, and the story loses a great deal of its clarity and force.
He blames the child, now a man, along with the others for his
sad life. Animal rage at pain is all that motivates his following
them and making his wife explain to the young man who he is
and why there is some dispute as to whose son the young man is.
Parent's decision to wallow in self-abuse and self-destruction for
the rest of his life now, at the moment when there are other
courses open to him, leaves the reader confused as to whether
old age or revenge motivated it.

It is Maupassant's inconsistency in attitude toward Monsieur
Parent that is the story's great weakness. Many critics fail to see
that in protesting against Maupassant's proclivity for telling the
same story again and again, they are condemning a phenomenon
which indeed in some is a grave fault, but which in Maupassant's
case is responsible for a substantial number of his great pieces.
He was not like his master, Flaubert, who could brood upon a
subject without giving it utterance until he was ready to tear it
from his soul in its most perfect form. First and last, Maupassant
loved to tell the story that was on his mind at the moment. In
most cases, it is a good thing of which he did not succeed in
purging himself on first telling!

V   *Eight Out of Ten: Why the Score Is So High*

In *Le Petit* (1883) Maupassant describes his hero, Monsieur
Lemonnier, as a good man. But just as he had in *Monsieur Parent*,

the author condemns so strongly a sort of pathological blindness born of adoration as to make us aware that his intention is to chastise the cuckold's fatal weakness. Hence, the careful reader is again aware that a sentimental reaction to the cuckold's plight is the last thing Maupassant wishes to inspire in his many treatments of this major subject of his work. And it becomes more apparent that the repetition of the theme and the consistency of Maupassant's condemnation of the man and not the circumstance are born of the immediacy of the circumstances of his family life. Clearly, too, there is here evidence that repetition in Maupassant was more the phenomenon of an artist making progress toward a more perfect realization of both his ideas and artistic aims. But unfortunately he did also take certain poorly conceived stories and simply place them in his novels with no effort to transform them into art. This is why critics have condemned the repetitions and in some cases lost the patience required to follow a story in the process of its gradual transformation into one of his great achievements: transformed so completely, the work does not appear to be the ideal realization of an oft-repeated theme, but something else entirely. The triumph of the author's style obscures for all but the most persistent the sinuous road strewn with the wreckage of the imperfect attempts to achieve what has now been achieved.

Monsieur Lemonnier's love for his child is monstrously disproportionate and sick as had been his adoration of the mother who had died in childbirth. The picture of Goriot blubbering fondly over Delphine is no more exaggerated than Lemonnier's adoration. He spoils his son, Jean: "The father always gave in, granted no matter what" (XXVII, 27). In the background stands the familiar figure of the disapproving maid who will degrade him by being the one to enlighten him about the child's real father, who, as is also usual, had been a most warmly welcomed guest in the household. Lemmonier hangs himself, leaving behind a letter instructing his wife's lover to take charge of the child. This is not only a very contrived solution, it is a rather cheap one. But Maupassant was a practical man, and he knew what the public wanted. The tragic suicide does not, however, dilute the bitter cup of Maupassant's contempt for the cuckold. In the mind of the critical reader the author's condemnation of the victim is as strong as ever.

Maupassant never assumed that a man was not being cuckolded as his familiar assertion in *Lui?* that 80 percent of the husbands are cuckolds demonstrates. There is every reason to assume that Maupassant was torn between a desire to see his own father punished by cuckoldry and a desire for his own mother to remain the superior, ideal paragon of virtue associated with the common idea of motherhood. That is why in *Une Vie* he likely had Laure de Maupassant in mind when he created Jeanne, who provides us a rather intimate portrait of what he regarded as a noble, if naïve, mother. Maupassant believed that any cuckold deserved his fate for having freely accepted the bonds of marriage. Not having embraced his philosophy "that free love is the only gay and good thing in the world" (XXVII, 27), they had brought about their own damnation. The state of marriage appealed to him only later, when he began to experience the terror of being alone in the night, and then only because it was a bastion against solitude. The idea is expressed in *Lui?* and recurs in numerous other places in his work. Despite his cynical assertion that 80 percent of France's husbands are being cuckolded, he seems at times to have yearned to be included in the majority. Old age and loneliness had become far more frightening to Maupassant than his youthful contempt for the weaknesses of the members of his own sex, and with his inability to find any other male companion who could replace Flaubert, he was tempted to seek companionship, for the sake of companionship, from a female. Just as his madness altered his writing and was the living reality that inspired several of his finest stories, it also altered his manner of viewing things: gone was the priority he had once given to defying the conventions that men accepted in lieu of the responsibility of being first men, of acting forcefully. His heroic qualities were victimized by fears of the hallucinations which might torment him in the long, lonely life of the celibate, and not by the general defeatism that ground away the heroic spirit of the French as the aftermath of France's defeat by Prussia. With this change in his life, Maupassant's scorn for the man who would sell the birthright that entitled him to dominance instead of subservience diminished.

VI   *In the Tradition of the Fabliau*

Cuckoldry is treated with the verve and humor of the fabliau but rarely. The best example of the droll treatment is *Un Sage* in which the hero finds that his wife's continual demands on him as a lover are beyond his strength. Rather than kill himself copulating, and not able to resist the tormented desire of his aphrodisiac wife—"She's that way because nature made her that way" (XXVI, 171)—he takes the advice of a friend and entices another man to his wife's bed. "It was just too stupid to allow himself to be destroyed in that manner, in the end" (XXVI, 176). *La Porte* (1887) is similar in tone and plot. Maupassant also treated the situation of the willing cuckold with gloomy gravity. In the case of Monsieur Lesable of *L'Héritage*, allowing himself to be cuckolded is the only manner of satisfying his tragic, insatiable greed. Pathological cupidity is not a disease with which Maupassant is sympathetic; greed is too base a trait, one which is too typical of the pettiness in man that Flaubert inspired him to loathe. In line with his contempt for man's weakness in allowing himself to be subservient either to his own desires or to the treachery of women, Maupassant describes his wretched hero as making himself ill in vain attempts to impregnate his wife in order to collect an inheritance which will legally be diverted to charity if there is no child heir. His wife is bitter and scornful of his lack of "manliness." His father-in-law who had, himself, hopes of getting hold of the fortune, lords his own former potency. Maupassant's desire to debase the typical male in general may be seen in Lesable's degradation: the wretch is lowered to the vulgar mockery of his peers in the naval office, goaded by a bully-braggart, a former rival, into a duel, then humiliated by his wife for agreeing to call off the duel, hounded by her and his father-in-law's reproaches, and finally forced to accept the reality that it is his bitter enemy who will perform the needed impregnation. His cruel intent toward the male victim is clear, but, in this case, so is his interest in showing the pettiness of woman, whose cupidity reveals her as an insufferable social hypocrite without a grain of appreciation for the man who had collaborated successfully in presenting a legal heir nor any compunction at turning up her nose at those who have been caught at her game. Maupassant depicts man here as an oppressively small creature.

The Homais-like character, M. Sacrement, of *Décoré* was obsessed with the desire to be decorated. Very much like Homais, he was continually seeking to place his name before the great by engaging in pompous and stupid ventures on behalf of his fellow creatures. But unlike Homais, he did not possess the crass callousness of the born small-town bourgeois politician necessary to persevere in masquerading failure for success long enough to force a weary officialdom to weaken and bestow the sought-for honor. Lack of the shrewdness of his Flaubertian parallel leads to his becoming a cuckold. And, as in the majority of cases, Maupassant is fiercely dedicated to destroying any sympathy one might have for a cuckold and inspiring instead a sort of cynical, degrading commiseration for the pitiful weakling cowering behind the masquerades of the master, the father, and the stronger sex. The hero returns unexpectedly and almost catches an official in bed with his willing wife. The two lovers, in order to hide their cuckoldry, convince him that the purpose of the official's visit was to present him with the long-desired medal. Later comes the ironic citation: "for exceptional services" (XXVI, 253). Rarely is Maupassant more grim in smashing the hero with a sort of Dostoevskian, Gogolesque brutality.

Maupassant's idea that the superior woman had a right, almost a duty, to cuckold a husband *who accepted the married man's right to have mistresses and frequent prostitutes,* is forcefully presented in *Au Bord du Lit.* That his father made no bones about playing with other women did not set well with Maupassant.

Maupassant's gallery of cuckolds also includes the one who lowers himself by being so naïve as to be incapable of calling a spade a spade. M. Lougère (*L'Assassin*) receives little but his creator's scorn for allowing himself to be dominated by his wife's lie to the point of killing his employer when the latter reveals the truth to him; he kills his boss out of pride and adherence to the convention that no honorable man would permit his wife to be slandered in such a manner. The fact that M. Longère's first wife had been a model of purity and that he had been raised completely sheltered from suspecting the possibility that there were among his fellow men and women those who were not bent upon treating their neighbors in the most kind and forthright manner did not excuse him in Maupassant's opinion; rather it drew from the author a withering contempt. The story is a model of that Realistic truth which arises from the proper arrangement of details by a master artist whose presence is everywhere but whose personal opinions are never seen. Flaubert would have approved heartily. However, the artistic achievement may be but a new reason Maupassant discovered for continuing to express no sympathy with males who set themselves up to be cuckolded, for whatever reason.

VII   *Woman—The Sacrificial Marriage Victim*

One is struck by Maupassant's sympathy for the woman who had been the victim of the customary convention which allowed fathers and mothers to decide whom their daughters were to marry. *(Madame Parisse* is a sympathetic defense for the title character's cuckolding of her husband; he had not wooed and won her but had been given her through family agreements.) Clearly such a social injustice caused him to side with the defenseless woman, to suggest that those who forced a young girl into cuckolding her husband—himself a willing accomplice—were to blame. And just as evident is Maupassant's conviction that man is not without defense against cuckoldry and so deserves no pity for weakness. Here, then, is another explanation for his continual refusal to sympathize with the cuckold.

Irony begins with the strange pronouncement of one of Maupassant's most famous cuckolds, M. Roland, Pierre's father in *Pierre et Jean*: "I invite women because I like to be with them, and then, *the moment I feel the waters beneath me, I think of nothing any longer but the fish*" (italics mine) (XI, 2). All of his life M. Roland had taken his wife and the husband's privilege for granted so that it is little wonder that he could dismiss women from his mind the instant he entered into an activity where their presence was unnecessary, and it is little wonder too that he had aided and abetted his own cuckoldry. Before retiring to Havre, the jewelry business in Paris had commanded all of his attention. His complete surrender to business with its consequential shortchanging of his wife had much to do with her turning to another man for attention. And as the book opens, M. Roland continues to enjoy his retirement by the sea to the utter neglect of his wife's feelings.

The brilliance emanating from Maupassant's deep penetration of male psychology blinds one momentarily to the fact that the two brothers share their father's guilt of having taken Mme Roland for granted. Even the sensitive and perceptive Pierre had been unable to imagine that the conventional role of mother and wife might not satisfy completely her yearning to be an individual. And so, though he is the first male to learn the truth, he too is a candidate for cuckoldry. The violent trauma that accompanies each shred of damning evidence against his mother demonstrates how insensitive he is to the emotional woman behind the conventional, rational one. Here, as everywhere in his writing, Maupassant is concerned with pointing up the kind of blindness he sees as typical of the male race which, by its insensitivity, contributes to its own cuckoldry. Instead of recognizing a woman's right to escape the entanglements of male-ego-inspired conventions, man but gives vent to outraged cries.

Strong evidence of Flaubert's influence upon Maupassant may be found in the latter's handling of Mme Roland's psychology and, as well, in the fact that *Madame Bovary* deals with cuckoldry. In this and a subsequent study I intend to examine evidence of more extensive literary influences than previously suggested by critics which are perhaps of far greater importance than the fatherly influence Flaubert exerted upon his disciple. Witness the thoughts of the woman who has a secret heart into which her husband has not peered, which indeed his stereotyped thinking prevented him from supposing existed. While M. Roland is enthusing over the ship *Normandie* which has just set sail from Havre, Mme Roland's active imagination clears all the hurdles: "she knew the price of money, which nevertheless did not prevent her from engaging in the *charms of dream. She loved reading, novels and poetry, not for their artistic worth but for the melancholy and tender revery they awakened in her*" (italics mine) (XI, 13). This vivid glimpse of her thoughts is enough to identify her kinship to Emma Bovary. There can be no question as to why Madame Roland broke the conventions that other women with equally indifferent and self-centered husbands, or worse, would nonetheless refuse to break. Maupassant reveals in this one scene how all of the prior treatments of the cuckolder of her husband were preparation for this ultimate one.

M. Roland merits his cuckoldry. The news of his friend's death only incites his cupidity. He is beside himself with joy at the prospect of Jean's receiving such a large inheritance of which he intends to get a slice for himself. Mme Roland, whose hopes showed a greed sharpened by the grinding stone of daily misery, turned instantly to sorrow when she learned whose death was responsible for the windfall. How loathsome is M. Roland's delirious joy mingled with his insensitivity and bland lack of imagination! "By Jove, he used to spend every evening with us at the house. And that's right, the morning John was born, he was the one who went to fetch the doctor" (XI, 35). Heavy, too, is the irony which reveals that the only sensitivity possessed by any male in the book is Pierre's, clearly an inheritance from his mother.

Jean is more like *père* Roland in his dullness, which indicates, perhaps, that Maupassant's intent was to show that the dead man as a hero and idealistic male existed only as a figment of Mme Roland's yearning imagination. She, in turn, had passed her sensitivity and determination to strive against convention on to Pierre, whose violent sense of outrage she and she alone sensed and understood.

One cannot but speculate that Maupassant's ability to plumb the depths of Pierre's conscience results from the close proximity this story has to his own relationship with his mother and father. And his understanding of the woman's psychology is a strong indication of how long and carefully he had considered his mother's influence upon him. Though Mme Roland yearned for the unattainable love Emma Bovary sought, she did not view her real-life situation as a temporary necessity, as did Emma. She, like Maupassant's mother, had learned to respect the irrevocable power of reality. This made her aware of the people and scene around her as something far more than just extensions of her own imagination, as the mere backdrop for her dreams. Hence Mme Roland perceived immediately what the fact that Pierre had been left out of the will would lead to. Maupassant shows her as a woman worthy of something more out of life than a faded marriage certificate forgotten in some drawer. Revealing how she attempts to prepare to deal with Pierre after the shocking discovery she knows he will make, Maupassant identifies her with those rare women whose personal magnetism causes us to be drawn to their side and to view their shortcoming as insignificant. Madame Roland's faults are indeed small beside the criminal insensitivity, lack of love and greed of the man whom convention would have described as a good husband and father.

Clearly one can gain a more substantial understanding of Maupassant's relations with his mother by studying *his work*. A critical biography of Maupassant that does not suggest how the themes of his writings were enhanced, magnified, exaggerated, or stunted by his own life experience merely contributes to an already large mountain of largely repetitive Maupassant biographies. In this most finished of his treatments of cuckoldry, one sees better than elsewhere how very real this problem was to Maupassant himself.

The sea was for Maupassant and for his characters, Pierre and Jean, a place for measuring one's strength. Strangely it is Pierre, whom any biographer of Maupassant would readily recognize as more similar to the author, who measures up badly in comparison to his brother. Jean is more reminiscent of Maupassant in physique; but in that far more important area, the intellect, it is clearly Pierre who utters the words and thinks the thoughts close to those of the author. The lines binding Maupassant to the older brother, moreover, are far more direct: Pierre suffers whenever he thinks of the relationship between his father and his mother, in much the same way as Maupassant suffered when he thought of his own parents' relations. Pierre is highly sensitive and fragile because of his sensitivity. Maupassant understands Pierre's fragility and so is able to share his understanding with his readers: the tumbling of Pierre's illusions about his mother whom he had until then regarded as the goddess of stability causes him to be left without something permanent to which to anchor his life. His experience is very much a part of the tragic human condition—man left without anything but himself to rely upon. Pierre's mother has long lived in dread of the probability that somehow she will not be protected by the conventional idea of the family which she had abused by her adultery. And yet one feels it is almost with relief that she finds herself deprived of the chance to shelter herself from her son's penetrating gaze. No longer will she have to be guilty alone, knowing that her son shares her secret. If she fears her son at first because she realizes how exactly his feelings of guilt and doubt and his sensitivity and capacity for silent, angry suffering mark him as her own flesh and blood, her fear gradually transmutes itself into the kind of ideal love she had experienced with her lover—a love that demanded not, but which resided in silent communion. Laure de Maupassant must have feared her son's acute sensitivity to the thoughts that her troubled marital life caused her in much the same way as Mme Roland feared Pierre's probing suspicions, but it seems that there was a tacit communication between them that thwarted the angry misunderstandings between mothers and sons that so often develop in such cases.

What strikes one immediately is how clearly Pierre's attitude toward the cuckoldry in his family reflects Maupassant's own attitude. That is, neither Pierre nor Maupassant is concerned with the cuckold, but rather each directs his major attention to the woman involved. Pierre rarely considers the cuckoldry he knows he is en route to discovering from the standpoint of its being an insult to his father. His entire attention in the matter is centered on his mother. He scorns the pettiness of his father's insatiable cupidity; he unleashes the furies of his intellectual snobbery upon his father—not on his mother: "Hadn't his mother been the voice of reason in the house?" (XI, 63). He considers M. Roland as unworthy of his consideration, as petty and stupid. This attitude is described by a man who need not depend entirely upon his imagination to develop the argument. One learns much of the author's mind's-eye view of Laure de Maupassant and Gustave de Maupassant by reading *Pierre et Jean.*

Mention can also be made of the fact that Pierre's sensitivity and intellectual excellence and Jean's blockheadedness closely parallel the major traits of Guy and Hervé de Maupassant. Pierre is spiteful in his malicious medical doggerel with which he attempts to intimidate and frighten his father out of celebrating with drinks. His scorn at how M. Roland and Jean snore as he agonizes over his by-now almost positive knowledge of the cuckoldry is reminiscent of Emma's for the sound of Charles's bestial snoring which infringed on her schemes to cuckold him. Pierre is so attentive to the wound of suspicion as to be unbalanced. Like all the chronically suspicious, he cannot conceive of the event as having any other consequence than its effect on him. He accepts nothing as real except as it affects him personally, denying the existence of that which does not affect him, and raising to demoniac proportions the idea that the universe has existed solely to conspire against him. Maupassant was able to plumb the depths of Pierre's psychology because he understood his situation so well. He said here what he would have said had the razor's-edge balance in his own family ever been lost so as to

call for such an outburst from him. Pierre, like Maupassant, felt
calm when he put out to sea; like his creator, he could always
see a bright future prospect for himself when busied with the
chores of sailing so that his thoughts were not of his mother's
past behavior.

On land he had to think his troubled thoughts: "He had to have
light shed on the matter, to be certain, he had to feel completely
secure in his heart, for he loved only his mother of all the beings
in the world" (XI, 96). The sounds coming to him from seaward
as he waits at his land listening post, with no sea to struggle
with, are the inspirers of troubled and confused thinking. Helpless
ships were feeling their way into the harbor, hoping for a beam
of light, just as Pierre, helpless and inactive, hopes for enlighten-
ment concerning his suspicions. His fantasy of what his mother's
dreams must have been that had made living only for a vulgar
man in a two-by-four shop impossible are remarkably like descriptions in *Madame Bovary:*

She had been young, with all the poetic weaknesses that trouble the
heart of the young! *Shut up, imprisoned in the shop next to a common-
place husband always talking business, she had dreamed of moonlight,
of voyages, of furtive kisses in the shadows of evening."* (italics mine)
(XI, 106)

And after this the conclusion that his mother had cuckolded her
husband is irrevocable.

The cruel pleasure Maupassant takes in making M. Roland a
blabbermouth, whose babble always succeeds in degrading him,
and showing his abysmal ignorance of how his friend had seduced
his wife erases here once and for all doubts concerning whether
the author felt any sympathy for cuckolded husbands. In regard
to the portrait of Jean's real father that Mme Roland had pretended to lose so that the resemblance would not be remarked,
Roland cries that no, he had seen her with it the other day which
must have been a presentiment of this good fortune. From first
to last his tongue disgraces him, marking him unworthy of any
worthwhile person's sympathy. When he tries to divine Pierre's
reason for mental anguish and for the sadness that has settled

over his household after the "good news," he discredits himself by jumping to conclusions with silly and facile bourgeois explanations. His wife's state of nerves he takes for some physical malady that Pierre ought to be able to cure. And meanwhile, *the cause of her mental suffering*, Pierre, "was looking at her like a judge satisfied with his task" (XI, 142). The obvious does not occur to the wretched M. Roland.

Pierre's ambivalent desire to forgive and to damn his mother threatens his sanity. Maupassant's ambivalence in his attitude toward women is reflected in the son's torment. Always, the center of interest remains the conflict between mother and son. Pierre views the upcoming marriage between his fortunate brother and the widow, Mme Rosémilly, as the preparation for cuckoldry, since for him as for Maupassant all husbands are cuckolds. Mme Roland defends the widow as a woman of unquestioned virtue and then suffers Pierre's sneering implication that she too has always been so regarded. When in a furious fit of malicious jealously and anger Pierre tells Jean the truth about the latter's inheritance, only to discover that his mother has overheard his tirade, he cries out against himself for having so cruelly hurt her: "Well, I'm a swine for having said that" (XI, 177).

The mother knows how ephemeral is the sympathy of ordinary men. Jean's holding her close and assuring her of his abiding love and protection draw from her a sad commentary: "You're weeping tonight, and tomorrow you'll be the first to throw me out" (XI, 183). She knows, too, that men are niggardly with their pardon when it comes to "fallen women." Her understanding of her younger son's weakness and dependence—not her desire to be accepted and protected—is all that makes her agree to stay with him. Pierre's refusal to forgive her has broken her heart and disillusioned her about men in general. She admits to Jean that she has no shame for what she has done and tells him that her staying with him will mean he must be willing to look the world in the eye and tell it he is another's son. Her description of her suffering beginning with the instant she suspected that Maréchal, Jean's father, no longer loves her is moving testimony to Maupassant's sympathy and respect for women who have been driven by prearranged marriages and insensitive husbands to find love and understanding elsewhere. Her utter dejection at man's failure to

measure up to the ideal in life comes to the hopeless pronouncement: "How wretched and deceiving life is!" The cry is strangely
similar to Emma Bovary's at her life's end. Mme Roland is afraid
of Pierre and has to look to Jean for protection, to Jean who possessed none of Pierre's dignity, who was hurt by the news of his
parenthood only because it threatened his bourgeois interests and
plans! Maupassant's contempt for him is clear and in evident contrast to his admiration for Pierre. Of Jean he says: "he also experienced at certain times this imperious need for immediate
solutions which constitutes the entire strength of the weak who
are incapable of persevering in their wishes" (XI, 194–95). He
easily "resigns" himself to accepting the fortune and to seeing that
Pierre is packed off, out of his life. Thus, it is his bourgeois
shrewdness that inspires him to suggest that his brother, already
the desperate prey of usurers, take the position of medical officer
on a ship about to be launched. The conflict between Mme Roland and Pierre has grown cold, but in its ashes the mother sees
that it had to flame furiously because she and her older son were
so much alike, so sensitive, so worthy as to have understood the
real meaning of love. "Le pauvre garçon," she mutters tenderly
and wistfully of Pierre who has to leave. "Life is villainous! If
one just once finds something good in it, he's guilty if he abandons
himself to it and he pays dearly for it later on" (XI, 208). Maupassant does not fail to reinform us that the greatest loss of all for
Mme Roland is the loss of the son whose violent love and idealism
she also feared.

For Pierre, as for Maupassant, the sea represented a means of
escape. But Pierre envisaged it as a prison to which his mother's
adultery had condemned him. But in that prison where there
would be no temptation and nothing to distract him but his work,
he would do what he had to. Maupassant understood what it
meant to be a person for whom the unfettered life offered comforting distractions and excuses that discourage even small efforts to
reach an ideal and for whom incarceration was the only chance
for salvation. Pierre wanted desperately to cause someone to shed
a tear over his departure. We see a terrible irony in Maupassant's
closing descriptions of his characters: M. Roland, as in the beginning raving over the great ocean liner from his small boat:
"And Mme Roland bewildered, half out of her mind, stretched
her arms out toward it, [the ship] and she saw her son, her son

Pierre, wearing his ribboned cap, throwing goodbye kisses to her" (XI, 240). Mme Roland understands the enormous irony that her life is disappearing with the ever diminishing speck of a ship on the horizon and that she will return to vegetate with her husband and other son.

CHAPTER 3

Maupassant's Women: His Mother and His Heroines

I The Growth of a Favoring Prejudice

MAUPASSANT was not showing us a Romantic "femme
fatale" when he repeatedly told tales in which the woman
gained ascendancy over the man. His admiration for woman
grew out of personal contact and observation, not from fear inspired by a superstitious cult. Among the strangely few men who
enjoyed Maupassant's unstinting admiration, most had chosen
celibacy and so were relatively safe from acts of weakness that
so often characterize a husband's behavior and which would have
lowered them in his esteem. Flaubert, of course, was so far in the
vanguard of this select few as to be the god of the microcosm.

To Maupassant, marriage was a form of servitude which the
female refused to accept because she recognized it as such, and
to which the male submitted while deluding himself with the
notion that he was free, the master. The calm demeanor and un-
flinching resolve of Maupassant's mother inspired early his admiration for woman and caused him to question the myth of
male superiority. Madame de Maupassant's influence upon her son
can never be accurately evaluated, for the more one ponders his
work the more one is struck with her presence in the character
of heroine after heroine. Far more accurate assessments can be
made of the influence of Maupassant's father in shaping the son's
prejudicial view of husbands as self-centered weaklings who deserved cuckolding, and of the role his disappointment in his
father had in determining him to seek in Flaubert a father who
was not weak or unworthy of the charge.

Paradoxically, we find Maupassant writing, near the end of his
days, in favor of marriage. The cruel spark of loneliness ignited
this twilight mania in a man who had spent most of his career
satirizing or openly denouncing the institution. Celibacy con-

firmed the strange and haunting terror that was typical of Maupassant's bouts with insanity. He speaks of his terror of loneliness in a letter to his mother: "I fear the arriving winter, I feel alone, and my long, solitary evenings are sometimes terrible. Often when I'm alone seated at my desk with my lamp burning sadly before me, I experience such complete moments of distress that I no longer know where to turn" (IV, cxxvii).

It should be stated that Maupassant did not always write with the aim of inciting sympathy for the married woman's plight or of excusing her extramarital affairs. *Une Famille* typifies a number of stories whose aim is clearly to decry how marriage destroys friendship between old male cronies and to express his repugnance at how the wife is always certain to drag her husband down to her level. However, these stories, with their strange male prejudice, lack the power of those which speak with admiration of woman. What vitality they have results from a sudden and ephemeral anger, and not from the slowly nurtured conviction that lends the moving power and lasting vitality to his writings which praise woman.

II *War Demonstrates Woman's Superior Courage*

The magnificent courage and nobility of woman in time of war and defeat inspired what many consider to be his greatest story, *Boule de Suif*. War was a fact of Maupassant's life. This makes his praise of woman's behavior as contrasted to the less admirable, often even cowardly behavior, of her counterpart the more striking. But it does not seem out of character to the one who has opened his eyes to the apparent philogyny in his other works. Philogyny is not merely a tone in Maupassant, it is the basic trait of his attitude concerning the human species.

The prostitute Rachel, in *Mademoiselle Fifi,* behaves in the way that epitomized for Maupassant the *effective* disdain of the conquered. Women can deal with a derisive effectiveness above man's capacities, Maupassant believes, because their long-suffering experience as prisoners of male conventions has taught them the mastery of derision. "You think you're raping the women of France," sneers the proud Rachel to the sadistic Mlle Fifi (Wilhelm d'Eyrik), "As for me! Me! I'm not a woman, *I* am a whore, that's indeed all the Prussians need or deserve" (X, 23). Her stabbing of him and the ringing of the bells which had remained

silent in the face of his ironic threats to have the townsmen's
blood or be the cause of their ringing again are almost anti-
climatic, following as they do in the wake of her success in making the Prussian feel the littleness ascribed to him and his kind
by those he had conquered but could not break.

The Comtesse de Brémontal's sensitivity, in the unfinished
L'Angélus, her love of poetry and her melancholy surroundings
are all reminiscent of Laure de Maupassant. Abandoned too by
a husband whose seignorial, Norman bravado presents to his
whimsical mind the going off to serve as a higher calling than
remaining with his pregnant, defenseless wife, the Countess behaves with disdainful composure in the face of threats by the
Prussian officer who has taken over her house. So effective is her
contempt that the Prussian suffers the ignominy fatal to all conquerors' pride. Maupassant had great plans for this novel to be
entitled *L'Angélus.* It was to be his masterpiece in the genre.
His dedication to the project and the magnitude of the idea he
had in mind can be guessed at from notes sketching what was to
follow the events described above: the Countess' boy child would
be born on Christmas a cripple in one of the château's outbuild-
ings, his disfiguration the result of his mother's having been
brutalized by the Prussian. The religious sources are perhaps a
little too obvious, but it must be kept in mind that the story came
to him as something that had to be written only when he was
already hopelessly in the grip of his tragic malady. No one can
say what turn he might have given the theme had he been in
good health.

The tragic fate of the lovely Irma of *Le Lit 29* has none of the
mawkish sentimentality of so many stories of its kind. While
showing us how war so tragically truncates those seemingly perfect love affairs, Maupassant demonstrates how it is the male's
weakness and imperfections that are really responsible for their
failure. The lady killer, Captain Epivent, was happy to rattle his
medals truculently against an enemy who had had the gall to
rape his woman and then take her life, and to hurl threats toward Germany in case of any future incursion. But when he
found that his beautiful former mistress was alive and had
syphilis, it was another matter; for in order to protect the noble
image of himself he sought to foster he would have to go through
the troublesome formality of paying her a solicitous visit. The

visit began on an ironic note which demonstrated clearly the selfless contrast of her love for him: she expressed pride in his medals and avoided complaining about her own wretched condition. Only when he pressed her did she reveal the patriotism that had prompted her to refuse treatments for the infection a Prussian had brought her: she had taken it upon herself to spread the infection amongst the hated army of occupation, using her beauty as a lure. It was what she could do to avenge her country's lost pride. She had known she would end up here, but it had been worth it. "And I also infected all of them, all, every single one, the most I was able" (XXIX, 82). The Captain left with the intention of never returning. But he could not play the hero before the people. Though he ignored her letter of entreaty, he had to go to save face when the hospital chaplain came after him.

Maupassant's description of her contempt for her former lover removes any doubts as to his dedication to emphasizing the sharp contrast between the pusillanimity of the male with his illusory strength, and the strong courage of the female with her alleged frailties. Irma's choice of a name for the man she was dismissing was forged in the mind of a creator burning with a sense of outrage at men blinded to the truth by their stubborn, ego-inspired antifeminism. "get away from me, *capon*! More than you, yes, I killed more of them than you, more than you" (italics mine) (XXIX, 88). She died the following day.

Berthine of *Les Prisonniers* is a healthy peasant girl whose vengeance against the invaders is blunt, unsophisticated, and as final as a wily Norman peasant's business transactions. She allows them in her house, tricks them into her basement from which escape is impossible, and then convinces them that surrendering to the local constabulary, ignominious though it may be, is the wisest choice for them. Evidence that Maupassant did not deem a male capable of this sort of clear design and execution is the fact that he presents an exceedingly satirical and damaging picture of the ostentatious, bungling militia commander who joyfully accepts total credit for the capture.

One sees the same admiration for the concise manner in which women exact their vengeance against the enemy in the story about the madwoman—insane with grief because she had befriended the Prussians, being an innocent in politics, until she

had learned their army had killed her son—and how she be-
guiled her Prussian "guests" into affixing their signatures to a
document before incinerating them in her house as they slept
soundly, sure of her friendship. She wanted their signatures as
proof to their loved ones that they were dead and that *she* and
she alone had been responsible for their deaths. Her steady dedication to her purpose is the quality with which Maupassant often
endowed his women: it is consistent with his depiction of woman
as uniquely capable of the kind of discipline necessary to over-
come the greatest obstacles.

III   Boule de Suif

The high place *Boule de Suif* occupies in French literature is
merited, for it presents with almost unparalleled power woman's
courage and resolve to survive defeat and personal degradation.
This story provides the clearest and most moving presentation of
Maupassant's admiration for female strength in times of dire disillusionment. Defeat breaks the souls of most of the men it tries.
And even those strong survivors of the initial shock, upon viewing the tragic shambles of their fellow beings' broken spirit, often
knuckle under to despair. The very few who can look upon defeat and its waste and still remain whole are the real heroes who
cause others to pick up their pride and begin again. A person
familiar with Maupassant's life and work will know why he
chose a prostitute for this almost superhuman accomplishment.
But one must see his treatment of woman in the proper light and
must be familiar with every line he wrote about her to reconcile
his ambivalence regarding woman as a general class, for the
question continually arises as to how he could have set a course
in his own life which seemed oriented upon degrading her. We
must conclude that the women he met in the bordello he found
to be the consummation of all the qualities he considered important and admirable: we have Boule de Suif as evidence. It is also
quite evident that choosing a prostitute was the best way for
Maupassant to continue his effective needling of society's pride
in its conventions, in particular the ones that tended to assign
a priori the virtues of acting heroically to the male and faint-
heartedness and ineffectual sentimentality to the female. And
even more pointedly he could mock the conventional stigmatizing
of prostitutes as socially destructive and morally inferior. The

lovely figure we see emerging from the wretched world that
spawned, abused, and reviled her, even giving her the derisive
name, Boule de Suif, to mock her, is the brainchild of a loving
and admiring creator, whose philogyny is evident.

Maupassant knew that the best milieu in which to test individual greatness was a world disillusioned with itself—a world
of defeat where wound-licking is often the last vestige of struggle.
Boule de Suif comes upon a scene where people are more concerned with adapting to defeat and calling it by another name
than with refusing to be servile. It is a world where her refusal
to accept the defeat the others took for granted both sets her
apart from the common herd and brings her into conflict with it.
She would not have been able to utter their eloquent idealistic
clichés, but she possessed idealism and the courage to pursue it.
Maupassant wastes no time in stamping her with the mark of
superiority. The coach has scarcely begun its journey before his
concise artistry has revealed to us that the other passengers, and
especially the women with their conventional morality leading
at best to the delusion of the rectitude of their ambitions for
peace and material prosperity, are indeed impoverished human
spirits with whom this brave, engaging prostitute contrasts
sharply. The author thus wins our esteem early and causes us to
be more wary of the others.

Loiseau, the wine merchant, spouts the kind of clichés typical
of the articulate among the society with which Maupassant found
himself at loggerheads. His pronouncement which removes the
other women's hypocritical compunction against accepting food
from a prostitute is the type of thing one finds in Flaubert's
Dictionnaire des idées reçues. And Boule de Suif's ignorance of
their absurd clichés sets her above them in our minds. Her
fellow passengers are shown from the beginning to be people
with nothing for the desperate times but talk. Boule de Suif
would never articulate the accepted idea that "in such cases all
men are brothers and should aid one another," but she would so
act. Maupassant with this brief incident has shown us the larger
meaning of his story, and how the meaning of his story tran-
scends the boundaries in which he had given it light. He could
not have been more effective in drawing the line between the
others and Boule de Suif. The latter returns what she takes from
life and more, and in so doing she is neither a conventional

prostitute nor a conventional human being; she is a woman and a superior human being.

Later, at the inn, in the scene in which the other traveling companions quarrel over what they think would be the right thing for Boule de Suif to do, the latter herself has figuratively ascended to an empyrean where the pettiness of her erstwhile companions is not permitted to trouble her deliberations upon her course. Maupassant shows considerable artistry in the symbology of having Boule de Suif upstairs in the inn, separated from the others physically by some *small* distance, while the distance of her spiritual separation is so vast, as vast as the distance between positive and negative. With the use of this symbol the author is able to reemphasize what he is saying with the whole story. The terrible pettiness of rationalizing to which we all resort brands itself upon our minds as they deliberate: "Since that's what the slut's trade is, to do that with any man, I find she has no right to refuse one anymore than another" (IV, 56–57).

Maupassant makes us see the real question that we all must face with such startling clarity that we know we are in the presence of a master. Through Boule de Suif's unerring understanding of what it means to give herself to the enemy, we come to understand what it means for us to give ourselves to the enemy. And, moreover, we learn that most people in giving themselves to everything give themselves to nothing and that the enemy will settle for nothing but the greatest individual as his price. Maupassant, like us all, mourned in the face of the realization that so often the sacrifice of the greatest only causes those who benefit from the selfless act to respond by a show of their utter unworthiness. He chose a woman to show us his admiration for the unique strength of the great. And as if to dismiss the male race from consideration for such a role, he depicts the self-anointed revolutionary and the only one of the other travelers who hesitates to throw Boule de Suif to the wolves, as incapable of action when it counted. He talks: "I'm telling you all, you've just done an infamous thing!" (IV, 69). And the next day Cornudet, the revolutionary, eats with the others from whom only inefficacious words had ever separated him and continues deluding himself by singing the "Marseillaise." Maupassant thereby is able to register again bitter disappointment and cynicism regarding the behavior in general of his countrymen. If *Boule de Suif* is truly

Maupassant's masterpiece, it owes the honor to an insistent admiration for woman which receives its finest artistic expression and compression in the story. The theme is not new, nor does it end here. Philogyny is omnipresent in his writing.

IV *The Image of Laure de Maupassant*

Madame de Maupassant's fear that the very genius of which she was so proud would be the cause of an ever-widening gulf between her and her son, though it might have proven well founded, need not have tormented her. In Maupassant's creative output alone, her influence is apparent, more apparent than it was to either mother or son. She perhaps could not see her success for the troubling fantasies her mind served up to her as she watched him move restlessly about Europe and Africa and as she watched him become more and more a recluse because of his art and his illness. The novels especially provide us with portraits of women who closely resemble Laure de Maupassant. The problems they face and their superiority in dealing with them seem to have been inspired by his observations of his mother's life.

In *Notre Coeur* we see a bitter rendering of a situation which Maupassant must have viewed as but a slightly exaggerated version of one his mother had faced. He speaks of the heroine, Michèle de Burne: "Married to a well-mannered but worthless man, one of those domestic tyrants, before whom everything had to give, to bend, she at first had been wretched" (XII, 7). Like Laure de Maupassant, Madame de Burne was not the kind of woman who would permit herself to become a slave to the shallow ambitions and vanity of an inferior husband. The difference in the way Maupassant causes Madame de Burne to work out her problem is the fictional aspect; the forces that aggravate the problem, a complacent and indifferent husband and a social milieu bent upon justifying rules to make the superior accept what the mediocrity takes for good remain the same. The story is told with varying emphasis in the other Maupassant novels. Each time the solution is different. We see Maupassant following in the footsteps of his teacher, Flaubert, in undertaking a study of the series of environmental forces that encircle a kind of woman who, rather than surrender her own ideas of her happiness and destiny, will struggle dramatically if inefficaciously.

Maupassant's heroines resemble Emma Bovary because they are placed in identical situations, not because of the way they deal with them. That they do deal with them, either through a stoic acceptance of fact or by establishing themselves as mistresses of their social fate, shows how they are different from Flaubert's heroine.

When death removed Madame de Burne's primary problem, she vowed never again to compromise herself in marriage. But she needed men. She needed to dominate them and succeeded in doing so. Then André Mariolle (whose determination not to be compromised by love was quite as strong as hers) came into her life. A paltry investment of her emotions shattered his resolve to remain independent. This easy conquest resulted from the Maupassantian conviction that the male is the weaker of the sexes when it comes to achieving the destiny he has set for himself. Mariolle was a nonwriting talker about writing. Maupassant's male characters were more frequently talkers than doers. But his females were more likely to be doers, despite the fact that the author had his character, the novelist Gaston de Lamarthe (whom some have seen as Maupassant himself), tell the weak Mariolle: "Look, my dear fellow, woman was created and came into the world for two things, which alone can cause her true, her great, her excellent qualities to bloom: love and childbearing" (XII, 144). Maupassant was fond of dropping this line with acquaintances who took it as evidence of a misogynism which does not appear justified considering all of the evidence to the contrary. Lamarthe is probably closer to expressing his creator's conviction when he argues that the Realist-Naturalist novelist in suppressing the poetic quality of existence and dealing only with life's grim realities is to blame for woman's turning upon her weaker counterpart: "Nowadays, my dear sir, there's no longer any love in books, nor any love in life. You were the ones who invented the ideal, they [the women] believed in your inventions. Now you're only exponents of precise realities, and following you they have begun to believe in the vulgarity of everything" (XII, 146). How strongly this suggests Maupassant's great depth of understanding of both *Madame Bovary* and of the Realist-Naturalist movement in literature! Mariolle's failure to reach any of the admirable goals he had set for himself is a presaging of his surrendering of all of his male prerogatives. Maupassant's hatred for inadequacies in the male flows into the book with as much force as his admiration for the female's ability to turn the tables on an environment fostering the conventions that threaten her individuality. This dual emphasis is one of the book's weaknesses. The latter half of the book is crowded with analyses of Mariolle which make it more and more apparent that such a weak prize is hardly worthy of Madame de Burne's efforts and that any dramatic reversal in his conduct is unlikely. Maupassant gives us a bit of autobiography in reverse in the character of Mariolle. Speaking of his hurt he says: "The arts having tempted him, he did not discover sufficient courage to give himself entirely to any one of them, nor the persevering obstinacy necessary to triumph in it" (XII, 205). Are we to assume, then, that the author's success in the arts being the opposite to his hero's failure, his success with women was just as clearly the opposite? Probably so. But that scarcely is sufficient to justify our admiration for the novel. Mariolle's algolagnic relationship with a serving girl whom he called upon to read to him every night from *Manon Lescaut* evidences the strange, almost maniacal proclivity Maupassant developed in later years for debasing the male. He exaggerates to the boring degree. He had already done an excellent job of reducing man to a low state in his treatments of cuckoldry. Perhaps in so doing he had spent his artistic capacities to deal with the subject.

V Fort Comme la Mort

Fort Comme la Mort is the only novel of Maupassant that treats woman with disdain. The book is a dull one which describes how the hero Bertin, terrified by the thought of growing old, abandons his mistress, Madame de Guilleroy, and attaches himself to her daughter, Annette, as if he hoped to revitalize himself on her youth. Maupassant, as is well known, was inordinately troubled by the prospect of growing old. The novel's mediocrity is in part due to the lack of that proper artistic detachment which he was able to maintain with incredible efficiency in his stories about madness.

He had, as was usual with him, already told the same story before in *Fini,* a *"conte."* It is clear that Maupassant's first purpose in the novel was to study the problem of aging without stressing as a point of issue the weaknesses or strengths of the persons who were undergoing the process. Therefore, our sole purpose in mentioning this novel with its dependent and fainting female is to offer it as proof that Maupassant did write stories which were not *intentionally* philogynistic. But they were, for the most part, colorless and unconvincing in their misogyny. Bertin is, moreover, quite in character. He certainly cannot be offered as evidence of any erosion of Maupassant's general contempt for the males—not when he has to be taught that the idea that a man in his forties can play like a lover in his twenties is erroneous and that simply wishing not to grow old does nothing to change the fact. Maupassant was only too aware of how typically bourgeois this notion of Bertin's was and was so angered at having created such a character that he destroyed him. The hero's death is as unbelievable as the rest of the novel: he was run over by a coach. Maupassant, perhaps, would have been better off had he not written the novel.

VI   Mont-Oriol

Christiane Andermatt, the heroine of *Mont-Oriol,* another disappointing novel, represented a personification of the author's cry of despair over the growing conviction that there was no such thing as an ideal love or marriage. Though, as Sullivan suggests, it is the weakest of his novels, it provides still more evidence of Maupassant's admiration for woman. Here, more than in most cases, the admiring treatment of the heroine is resultant to Maupassant's failure to find much worth consideration in the man. She wins his praise by default, so to speak. If the "main characters are mere clichés, uninteresting as individuals," then it becomes apparent that a part of the blame for the bad book has to rest with his proclivity for presenting the female in an advantageous light. Christiane expresses Maupassant's own deeply felt disillusionment with the dream of two beings finding the ideal in each other, and in this role she is not without individuality.

when she had thought that their flesh and their souls constituted but a single flesh and soul, they had but scarcely approached one another, just close enough to cause the touching of their impenetrable envelopes in which mysterious nature has isolated and enclosed humans. *She saw clearly that no one had ever been able to break that invisible barrier which puts beings in life as distant one from the other as are the stars in the heavens.* (italics mine) (XVIII, 410)

Maupassant frustrates her by instilling in her mind the illusion that a great love is possible before shattering her hopes with the revelation that her lover, Paul Brétigny, in spite of his poetic idealism, is hollow and vain like all men. She is defended from those who would condemn her cuckoldry in typical Maupassantian fashion: Andermatt deserved it. The sarcastic tone of Maupassant's description of the Jewish financier, Andermatt, so clever in business and so wrapped up in deals as to be oblivious to anything else, is doubtless unworthy of his creative powers in its lack of originality. But Andermatt's blindness is not unlike that of M. Roland of *Pierre et Jean*. Both are totally incapable of conceiving the possibility of being cuckolded. And so Andermatt, too, accepts his wife's pregnancy with the faith of the complacent husband-stereotype and is no more obnoxious or lacking in individuality than is his counterpart in *Pierre et Jean*, a novel rarely accused of being clichéistic.

Here, as elsewhere, it is not the woman who is to blame for the failure to achieve the ideal union of two souls. It is Paul Brétigny with his cowardice and brutal indifference to her—once he discovers he is the father of her unborn child—who causes the dream to fail. Maupassant condemns the man who deals harshly with a woman, as he had condemned his own father. It is far from the author's intention to suggest that insisting upon his supposed rights of dominance is a firm, masculine act. His intention is rather to show us that his brutality and indifference are but male subterfuges.

Christiane's outcry at the instant she learns her baby is a girl recalls Emma Bovary: "Oh, my God!" (XVIII, 391). But she cannot abandon the baby because it is going to be subject to the prejudices and limitations imposed on it by a male-dominated society. And so she resolves to show Paul her sovereignty and then to dismiss him. Maupassant paints a cruel picture of the weak lover being denied even a glimpse of the baby. But his heroine, by the manner in which she demonstrates she has come to grips with her fate and has asserted her individuality, excites one's admiration. The men in her life are indeed but clichés, but she

remains in the mind as a symbol of Maupassant's philogyny, and
she makes one realize fuller the extent of Laure de Maupassant's
influence on her son's writing.

VII   L'Inutile Beauté

L'Inutile Beauté is an ironic title fashioned by Maupassant
expressing his anger with the stupid bestiality which had created
the conventions that made it a virtue to corrupt the beauty of a
woman and a crime for her to seek to defend it. The accepted
idea that it was a disgraceful and unnatural waste for a beautiful
woman not to bear children receives all the fury of a writer who
had been coached in contempt for the *"idée reçue"* by the master,
Flaubert. Maupassant's philogyny causes him to fashion the idea
that a woman's rebellion against the deformities of pregnancy is
more natural than unnatural, a dogma which for him was incon-
trovertible.

The story's heroine, the Comtesse de Mascaret, has set out to
prove that the supposed Holy Writ that declared a beautiful
woman was all the more required to perpetuate the species than
a plain one *had not* come from heaven but was a fraudulent
document forged by the male ego. The author's readiness to do
battle with this convention that came closer to being accepted by
the oppressed victims than any other male ordinance, and which
had received repeated anointings by religions shows that Maupassant was willing to risk everything in the cause of his philogyny. Maupassant was infamous for his frank emphasis upon
woman's utility as a means to sexual gratification and pleasure.
That he seemed to prefer her in this role to that of mother made
a great deal of difference to his critics, who pointed to his fre-
quenting of bordellos as a sign of a degenerate and corrupted life
and a crassness toward women. But to observe his actions merely
as the basis for drawing such criticisms is to miss the point: Maupassant had a genuine respect for the woman who sold her beauty
to give pleasure, which he saw as every bit as noble a sacrifice
as motherhood. It also followed therefore that a beautiful woman,
no matter what her station, had every right to oppose the legalized
annihilation of her beauty by a husband who cared only for his
immortality, his family name, and his pleasure. But many obser-
vers found Maupassant's behavior paradoxical to such a degree
that they could see little but hypocrisy in his defense of woman.

There is, however, no paradox, and to assume that there is obscures his message and makes it impossible to see such "*nouvelles*" as *Boule de Suif*, *La Maison Tellier*, and *L'Inutile Beauté* in the light required for a proper interpretation and a fitting of them into the overall scheme of his work.

Maupassant's scorn for the male plays a most important role in shaping the philosophy that produced *L'Inutile Beauté*. The hero's pusillanimous cry that the law is on his side achieves the purpose Maupassant intended: it makes us wonder if it isn't a shame that conventional marriage laws serve men who are so weak as to have nothing of a more noble cast to keep their wives at home. The *nouvelle* is a sober appraisal of a kind of dominant male to whom all laws which serve to assure his position of sovereignty are sacred, despite evidence that many of them may break higher laws which eventually will bring his civilization down upon his head. The Count of Mascaret's children interest him only as proof of the moments he had been master over his wife. His wife interests him mainly as an object to be dominated and left to vegetate. He is hence a perfect prey for her scheme to get even by telling him the children are another man's.

Maupassant's thesis in the story is an interesting expression of his esthetic idea that all beautiful things are the result of the imagination which is both mankind's unique blessing and greatest curse. A curse because it is the instigator of frustrated and endless searching for an ideal love; a blessing because it is the crowning glory of the work of a few great men worthy of elevating the status of mankind. To him the great irony is that the ones who discover and protect beauty are treated as miscreants, while the ravishers of it are supported by the pack. It is again noteworthy how Maupassant's admiration for woman places her not only in harmony with vital elements of his philosophy, but extends to her the role of representing them in his work.

VIII   Bel-Ami

The novel, *Bel-Ami*, has been much praised by critics. Its hero, Duryoy, seems to present a relief from all of Maupassant's males whose weaknesses draw his condemnation. But a close scrutiny of both the hero and its principal heroine, Madame Forestier, will vanish any notions that Maupassant's attitude toward the male and female has made an about-face. Madame Forestier, like

Maupassant's mother and the ideal woman we have seen portrayed elsewhere, lays down certain prerequisites for accepting a
proposal: "But it would also be necessary for a man to put himself to the task of seeing in me an equal, an ally, and not an
inferior or an obedient and submissive wife" (VII, 291). Bel-
Ami's ambition was responsible for his decision to marry the
widow of his publisher: such a marriage would assure his rise
in society. But he never enjoyed the supremacy over her which
custom allowed because his creator, even in describing one male
who managed to get his way in his life, was not willing to allow
him to be free of female superiority. Duryoy was never permitted
to forget that his success was due to the fact that he had been
her puppet: she wrote his best material. She was the ventriloquist
without which he had no voice. Even his co-workers derided
him. "You'd be nothing without her" (VII, 347). And as if to
make more certain the subservience of the male, Maupassant
enumerated the sufferings of his hero occasioned by the suspicion
that his wife was cuckolding him. Manifesting his desire to ex-
pose the male as weak and dependent in contrast to the female,
Maupassant showed that even his decision to divorce her is only
the hero's vain attempt to flee a superior woman's domination.
And he gave to him for a second wife a woman from the same
mold as Emma Bovary, one whose dreams, like Emma's, made
her an easy prize, not a conquest worthy of a heroic male:

Suzanne also dreamed; and the bells of the four horses jingled in her
head, making her envision an endless procession of highways spread
out in eternal moonlight, somber forests through which one passed, inns
at the end of the day's journey, and the host of stable boys waiting to
reharness their coach, for all knew that they were being pursued.
(VII, 540)

Though, as has been previously demonstrated, Maupassant
regarded marriage as an imposition upon the male, he was,
nevertheless, not in sympathy with the male's problems simply
because man held the option of changing the conventions regarding marriage and yet steadfastly refused to initiate a change. The
female received his admiration and sympathy because she had
no options. In Sur l'Eau, his attractive autobiographical sketches,
Maupassant makes it clear that he is firmly committed to demon-

strating how it is that woman is victimized by marriage far more than man and that he has none of the conventional admiration for the institution:

A priest using Latin authorizes with pontifical gravity the solemn and comical animal act which agitates men so profoundly, causes them to laugh so boisterously, to suffer so greatly, to weep so plentifully . . . the last rites for a virgin's innocence. (XXVIII, 102–3)

IX   Une Vie

The evidence of Maupassant's philogyny provided by the novel, *Une Vie,* is so obvious as to have caused a variety of critics to comment upon its appearance there. We have, therefore, saved the most conclusive evidence until the last. Saving it as the conclusion to a discussion of Maupassant's philogyny can also be justified by the novel's strong autobiographical coloring. From it a critical reader can piece together many of the puzzles that present themselves to the Maupassant scholar. It is no wonder that Maupassant's sense of moral outrage at the fact that nineteenth-century French society conspired to crush the vitality from woman and leave her stripped of the right to be an individual is so prominent in this *particular work!* The inspiration for it came in part from his observations of his mother's life. The attitudes expressed by the author in the novel magnify the influence that Laure de Maupassant had upon her son to the point that we cannot fail to consider it in criticizing his work.

The novel is set in the same general locale where Maupassant spent his childhood. The husband of the heroine of *Une Vie* has strikingly similar traits to those Maupassant silently resented in his father. And the air of hostility that developed between Jeanne and her husband is not unlike that which developed between Gustave and Laure de Maupassant. Viewing these obvious similarities between the situation in *Une Vie* and the one dominating much of Maupassant's childhood could lead one into the bog of oversimplification. We have, therefore, been careful in our choice of passages with the hope of shedding some further light on Maupassant's strange relationship with his parents.

It can be safely suggested that Jeanne's impatience to be released from the monastic school she had been attending derived from the emotions Maupassant himself experienced at being cooped up for several years in a private school. The manner in which he presents her thoughts at the prospect of escaping is too authentic not to have been inspired by memories of the Séminaire d'Yvetot. Jeanne's love of the sea gives Maupassant a chance to voice his own: "and she continually promised herself an infinite joy in that free life in the midst of the sea's waves" (II, 5). For Maupassant, too, the Elysian Fields were the moving waters.

The ghost of Emma Bovary hovers over Maupassant's description of his heroine's emotions regarding her future marriage:

They would go along, hand in hand, glued against each other, hearing each other's beating heart, feeling the heat upon their shoulders, mingling their love with the suave clarity of the summer nights, so united that they would penetrate, by the singular power of their tenderness, to the very depths of their secret thoughts. (II, 20)

This is Flaubert without the cold scorn, for as evident as is the master's influence, one cannot ignore the imprint of his mother's influence. Tolstoy praised the novel highly. And it is evident that his praise was inspired by the author's compassion and by the novel's lack of a deterministic-positivistic objectivity which certainly may be attributed to Laure de Maupassant's influence. Maupassant's emotional reaction to the situation in which he places his heroine is clearly resultant to his memories of life with his mother.

Jeanne's love of swimming and the sea is a manifestation of Maupassant's passion. When he describes her reveling in the presence of the sea, he is describing his own emotional response: "She felt sound and comfortable in that cold, clear, blue water which bore her out while supporting her" (II, 27). And later the author describes her: "and it seemed to her that three things alone were beautiful in creation: light, space, and water" (II, 46).

It was Maupassant's opinion that idealism should not be punished by shallow laws created by stupid men. To him it was sufficiently punished by nature. But Jeanne is, nevertheless, another victim of a system which, even given the good intentions of her parents, will deny her the privilege of finding an ideal husband. Her idealism is saddening, especially when we realize that Maupassant is describing a situation that was very close to him, one which he had sensed in the tragic relationship between his mother and his father. His outrage is again evident against a system which could cause a father to admonish his daughter: "but don't forget this, just this, that you belong entirely to your husband" (II, 82). There is no evidence that Laure de Maupassant ever capitulated quite so finally to her husband. There is, however, an indication that Maupassant based at least parts of his book, *Une Vie*, upon the life of his mother, and that the anger he expressed toward the system of masculine prerogatives that enslave woman was clearly inspired by his close touch with masculine tyranny in his own home. In this novel the frail shell of woman hides a great soul. The portrait of Jeanne is not unlike the one he bore in his mind of his mother.

Repeatedly Maupassant reveals his championing of the woman's cause. His philogyny is evident in the following lines, where he shows such sensitive sympathy: "And ceaselessly through the whole day, like an incessant rain so sad as to draw tears, these last leaves, now entirely yellowed, like great golden sous, were detaching themselves, spinning about and falling" (II, 118). The *"tristesse Verlainienne"* could not more movingly portray the desolation of Jeanne's life, chained as she was to a man who slept with the maid, lied to her about her own money, and with a disgusting show of self-righteousness condemned the maid in order to remove her and the baby, which he had fathered, so they would not disturb his tranquility. Like her creator, Jeanne's depressing condition drives her to hallucinations and to thoughts of suicide. But then there was hope: she was pregnant.

The child was a boy. She was certain he would dominate the world in which she had been a slave. Unlike Emma Bovary, she had not turned to the wall at the sight of the child. But Flaubert had been kinder to Emma; for he had not stirred her hopes. Jeanne's hopes for the boy became her life. Her husband continued to disappoint her by having an affair with a countess who had pretended to be her friend. What made this affair even more sorrowful for her was the fact that she admired the cuckolded husband who was brave and honest and a gentleman, the exact opposite of Julien. The affair drove her to conclude what Maupassant himself decided: "Everyone is perfidious, a liar and a phony" (II, 222).

Normandy, beloved of both the author and his heroine, where

she had once been so happy, seemed to conspire to augment her cynicism as it did in Maupassant's later life. Her weeping for her illusions caused her to draw more and more within herself. Her thoughts sound like Maupassant's own: "that sensation of emptiness, of scorn for man, she felt it increasing, enveloping her; and each day the petty, regional gossip inspired a deeper disgust in her soul, a stronger sense of shame for the human species" (II, 223). Her description of sex now is like the author's: "*sale bestialité.*" Jeanne is hence partly that elusive woman Maupassant never succeeded in finding in life, partly his mother. Her disgust with men's lack of idealism in love is just the print from the Maupassant negative. Both author and heroine were resigned to the fact that their idealism was inevitably doomed.

The irony of Jeanne's having been given a son becomes clear when Paul turns out to be a replica of his father, not the kind of young man able to accept his mother's pathetic kindness without repaying her in further suffering. Jeanne does not want to surrender him for even long enough to allow him to receive his schooling. One wonders what Laure de Maupassant thought when she read Paul's complaint. "I wasn't made for the obscure, humble life, sad enough to kill me, to which your tenderness seeks to condemn me" (II, 298). It is likely that at some moment or another Maupassant must have felt that way about his mother. But generally he was incapable of any but kind thoughts about her. Possibly because nature had equipped him with the kind of genius that made him capable of escaping whenever he chose, he never felt bitter over his mother's overprotectiveness. The case of his brother, Hervé, who may have been in the author's mind as he fashioned the character of Paul, was obviously quite the contrary.

Once away at boarding school Paul escapes and thereafter lives a life of dissipation that leads to a series of demands for money from his mother. The totality with which he destroys the last vestiges of his mother's hope becomes too melodramatic to be worthy of the rest of the book. Irony crosses irony in an endless tangle and her old age becomes filled with hallucinations born of her great loneliness—the same kind of loneliness Maupassant knew so well in his own last days. And as if foreseeing the aggravating force loneliness was to have on his malady, the author had the peasants of Jeanne's village referring to her as "*la Folle.*" She felt pursued by an obstinate demon who had created her solely for the pleasure of destroying her. Descriptions of her at the last are reminiscent of passages written by Maupassant during his last years to describe his hallucinations and loneliness: "she saw, as she had so often seen, her father and mother warming their feet by the fire" (II, 374). And the sentence describing her last view of the house has a haunting similarity to François Tassart's rendering of his master's final turn to catch a glimpse of his beloved boat, *"Bel-Ami":* "She felt in her heart that she had just said goodbye forever to her house" (II, 375). The book, ironically, does not end with her death but with a scene depicting her smothering Paul's girl-baby with kisses, overjoyed that its mother had died in childbirth. Maupassant's admiration for the madwoman who had taken all a cruel system had to offer and was still standing is an outstanding indication of his philogyny.

CHAPTER 4

The Gentle Sea

I *An Absorbing Passion*

IT would be unthinkable for the historian or critic of British literature to neglect the preponderant influence of the sea upon both the literature and the literary personalities under consideration. A study of Maupassant would be no less incomplete that did not take cognizance of the dominating influence of the sea and other bodies of water in the author's life and work. From childhood onward the sea represented a place of asylum, a place for renewal of his forces, a deity which awed him and called forth a reverence reminiscent of Homer or Melville. He loved the strong, coarse men of the sea. And though he saw the sea as the master who called forth the best in men, he also saw it as a capricious mistress who allied herself with the other sirens whose sole interest was in captivating strong men worthy of their attention: "It isn't just the perfidious sea that devours them thus, men. She has an all-powerful ally, one who aids her each night, in her greedy feast upon human flesh, alcohol" (IX, 267).

When he came to Paris with the dismal prospect of staying there for a long time, he found that he could restore some of the peace and harmony he expected of existence by becoming a fresh-water sailor on the Seine. He could not forgo the privilege of being near ships and waters and the people who made the water their home; that part of his life at Etretat he would not surrender. He had been tutored by sailors as a boy, and he missed the inspiration of the port and sailing as he squirmed in his desk chair at the Ministry. The inspiration had not only nurtured his literary bent but had given him the physical release which the energies of a powerful man needed. The only asylum he could find in the great city was its river. And fortunate it is, for the Seine proved to be one of his most fruitful sources of characters and stories. Here he observed weekend boating enthusiasts whose voracious sexual appetites and brawling natures were similar to those of the sailors (home from the sea) he had met at Etretat, and whose behavior he had been proud to imitate. He understood them and enjoyed telling of their exploits in the bordellos that were their favorite shoreside haunts. His understanding of them and enthusiasm for their vitality are at the same time the model for his own life style and the reason for the Realistic excellence of his stories in which they play a role.

But with all of his interest in the sea and rivers and in the people who drew their livelihood or pleasure from them, Maupassant showed little interest in presenting the struggle between man and the creatures of the waters. This is significant. For as any reader of Maupassant knows, he was most fond of tales about the struggle between man and the other creatures who share the land, and which he hunts for profit or the thrill of pitting himself against their strength. And yet there is little of the fear of the great unknown monsters of the sea or of a desire to challenge them. He seems to have viewed the sea and rivers, because the only men they beckoned to them were strong men for the most part bereft of the pettiness and foppishness of society, as rare places of peace and harmony.

II A *Lady of the Seine,* Mouche

Maupassant does not even appear to be trying to disguise the autobiographical in some of his pronouncements in *Mouche.* The *canotier*'s enthusiasm for the Seine is Maupassant's own: "My one great, absorbing passion for ten years was the Seine" (XXIV, 100). The extent of the Seine's influence upon his writing reaches its fullest in this story. His imagination is at its finest, and yet it is clear that the tale has been completely researched. Imagination and the Maupassantian Realism combine to become one of his finest *contes.*

Like many of his other stories this one grew in bits and pieces. There were other tries to tell a story with basically the same plot and certainly the same ideas and attitude toward the characters. But none had the exquisite poetic cast of *Mouche.* We have noted before how Maupassant was continually working toward the ultimate evocation of an idea and that these repeated attempts to do the same thing are rarely regarded favorably by critics. But perfection here makes an eloquent apology for his repetitive technique. And for the biographer the story provides a firsthand account of the things Maupassant came into contact with in his many visits to the Seine. He is describing men whom he knew and to whom he listened for pleasure and for ideas. Without doubt he knew a "Mouche."

The story describes five *canotiers* whose thought waves moved with as rhythmic a harmony as their paddles and their successful search for a woman to attract business and make them oblivious to the physical taxing of rowing their boat. A woman was indispensable to a boat, and their previous efforts had all ended unsatisfactorily. It took Mouche but a couple of days to conquer their doubts and then their hearts as she had those of their one-eyed comrade who had found her. A delightful alcoholic, she had them battling over the privilege of doing the most for her. And thus, her presence threatened the fraternal bonds that had held them together as a unit.

Maupassant had often studied the problem of how a woman could disrupt not only the monotony in the lives of the clerks and petty businessmen of Paris but also the harmony their interdependent slavery had nurtured in them. He had, without doubt, feared that he would find himself in a position where a startlingly different acquaintance or experience could tip the scales; for he knew what it was to be tethered to the monotonous sameness of a bureaucratic existence where even the hope for interruption eventually died and there was nothing left in the mind but a stubborn desire to defend stability as the end of existence. Fortunately he had his art. But he understood the problem as only one who conceives of himself as being caught by it can. In the case of his bureaucrats, harmony was never completely, if at all, reestablished.

But the author's fondness for the men of the waterfront prevailed over his doubts about man's more noble side. He endowed his oarsmen with unusual wisdom. (Or did he consider it to be unique with sailors?) They conquered their petty jealousies and resumed their harmonious style of life. Maupassant must have had a model for Mouche, so named because she too "always alighted upon carrion": her portrait shows that the author was as meticulous an observer of the behavior of waterfront women as he was of their male counterparts. Despite a sprightly ambiguity, she is nonethless a very real character. Maupassant created for her an ideal society over which she reigned rightfully as the strongest, most admirable member of all. Her wit and humanity brought out the best in her subjects. It is not surprising to those familiar with the matriarchal influence in his life that Maupassant allowed *her* to triumph.

Her pregnancy was inevitable, but when it became apparent, there was simply joy—not the usual male-ego-inspired battle over who was the father. Instead of displaying the inferior and destructive behavior that characterizes the rivalries that destroy harmony in society, these men decided to share the responsibilities and benefits of paternity equally. Their agreement is strange since it was recounted by a man who had continually written on the subject of uncertain paternity and who even had felt compelled to rebel against the means nature had of preventing a man from ever knowing for certain he had fathered his own child. Just as some of his best stories were inspired by his possibly exaggerated estimate of the prevalence of cuckoldry, one of his best was inspired by the certain knowledge that there were men in the world capable of sublimity. He found these superior beings to be men who had taken to the waters, men who must have been real to have convinced him to renege on the hard line he had adopted toward the male in the major part of his work. Maupassant did not lay claim to a resemblance to these men of *Mouche*. He was more an intellectual than a man of action. He would not have been a successful replica of Melville. He was like Flaubert and his mother, and like the French intellectual in general, he could draw more from vicarious experience than from the real thing. Being chained to those social rocks of civil servitude and the publishing industry, however, made him experience the kind of acute yearning to be a magnificent, heroic man of action. His art was a sort of pearl with which he surrounded the pain of disappointment at falling short of the heroic in life. Maupassant was a weekend sailor. He knew it, and the knowledge made him see more clearly the difference between sailors and ordinary men.

When Mouche nearly killed herself clowning in her usual manner a few weeks before the baby was due, the men responded in a manner still more noble than previously. They did not allow their disappointment that the baby was born dead to obscure the fact that Mouche's hurt was far greater than theirs and that she needed their unified love and help if she was to retain her sprightly sense of humor and mental health. Maupassant's rendering of their comfort into a few words which tell their love and simplicity so poignantly is an unusually simple illustration of the poetic power and Realism that combine in his works with such a unique effect: "Console yourself, sweet Mouche, we'll make another one for you " (XXIV, 116).

Mouche is unique among Maupassant's works. Nowhere else does he show such a balanced admiration for both the male and female of the human species. One can see that Maupassant was truly proud of belonging to the same race as these figures. The water, sailors and their women brought forth from him the few, infrequent rays of optimism.

III   *A Sea of Troubles,* Le Noyé

If the sea was capable of inspiring Maupassant to a rare optimism and enthusiasm for his fellow creatures, and a feeling of comradeship in the common effort against life's odds, it was also instrumental in causing him to exaggerate the strange manias that tormented him. *Le Noyé* has as its hero a fisherman whose wild temper and violent treatment of his women characterize the majority of Maupassant's waterfront men. But the attitude expressed in *Le Noyé* and elsewhere in Maupassant is more conciliatory and understanding toward the drink-enflamed husband who persecutes his family than the indignant reproach directed against such men by the illustrious master of Médan, Zola. Far from being indignant at the behavior of these drunks, Maupassant seems to have been attracted to them because of the obvious contrast they afforded with the character of the pale clerks of Paris with their infamous intrigues designed to gain ascendancy over their fellow prisoners.

The wife-beater of *Le Noyé* was lost at sea in a violent storm. The memory of his tyranny was so great, however, that his hag of a wife who had once been a voluptuous tavern wench could not accept his death. The air of dread and the interest in the supernatural that plagued Maupassant, that convinced him that he was pursued by beings set to destroy him, was never more present than in his stories about the sea. It is not surprising, then, that the wretched woman of the story became convinced that a foul-mouthed parakeet she had bought at an auction was the reincarnation of her cruel husband. One cannot ignore the probability that there is some significant hint of Flaubert's influence in that the story presents an interesting reversal of the heroine's attitude toward her parakeet from that of Félicité in *Un Coeur Simple*. In Maupassant the woman fought with the bird and killed it, but its hold upon her was clearly the same naïve, supernatural-religious-mystic attraction that had dominated the relationship between heroine and bird in Flaubert's story. Just as death's departing hallucination for Félicité presented the bird as a manifestation of the Divine to whose perch she had long before elevated it, Maupassant's heroine felt that she had killed more than a bird, that she was a sort of Judas with the blood of Christ on her hands: "then she came back into the room, threw herself on her knees before the empty cage, and distraught over what she had done, begged forgiveness of God, sobbing as if she had committed a horrible crime" (XXIV, 132–33).

The sea which was his favorite haunt in nature could restore his creative powers and calm him. But it had an unsettling influence upon Maupassant's imagination. As he became more and more misanthropic, seeking a hospitable environment on the sea away from society, he became more and more aware of and tortured by the sea's impassivity. Sailing on the sea or on the river became for him less attractive. But with the diminishing of his enthusiasm for them, it becomes evident that not only his health was declining but his power to discern in life the acts which most needed poetic expression.

IV *By the Beautiful Sea*

Maupassant loved sea resorts and their characters. Etretat was not dear to him solely because he had spent much of his happy childhood there; it was a gathering place for those who had enough money to loaf, fish, sail, and sun and for those who had nothing but a vague ambition to do these things and who had managed by luck to succeed. He wanted to be back among these types where he could study them. The financial independence that his writing finally afforded him had a profound influence on his life and work afterward. He bought "la Guillette" where he could study the gigolos, the confidence men, and the beachcombers firsthand. Out of his observations came such characters as Bombard who discovered that success in finding a woman to support his loafing came at the price of losing his freedom to be his own man. Maupassant had to be his own man. That is perhaps why in so many stories such as *Bombard* he attacked the idea of marriage. At heart he was a sailor, even if he was only part-time and unheroic in the role, and being his own man was very important to him. It was his contention that marriage subverted the male's right and duty to realize the state of freedom to which he was called. But Maupassant enjoyed observing and analyzing the case histories of the Bombards of the world whose desire to live well at sea resorts leads them to the incorrect assumption that marrying a wealthy but otherwise hopeless spinster will so stimulate her gratitude as to allow one to go on about his life as before, except with money. It is the kind of situation comedy that shows how much the heritage of the fabliau affected Maupassant. But the struggle and disillusion of these seaside gigolos of Maupassant cannot be viewed by a reader with the same goodwill and humor with which one can read the fabliaux, for always present in his tales of this sort is a shade of personal consternation at the fact that such strong men can lose their freedom, for whatever reason. The humor, then, is almost nonexistent.

Men of the sea, the river sailors and those who chose the seashore for their home were a breed apart in Maupassant's opinion, perhaps because his life was so much influenced by the water that he considered himself at one with them. Their resolute and stoic struggle to master nature, doomed as it was to failure, appeared glorious to him, and he admired their utter rejection of conventions as the behavior to be expected of Titans. Maupassant learned their language and developed a spiritual affinity with their stoic philosophy as a child at Étretat. One can hardly overemphasize the importance of his having grown up in their company. Both the tone and content of his literature would have been completely different without them and the locale that afforded him their companionship. If their influence is not felt directly in a story, it is almost always present in the nuancing of a certain character, an attitude, or an idea.

Maupassant's awe of the storm-enraged sea breaking upon some Norman fishing village is much akin to his awe of the power and violence of the raw men who fought with it for its bounty. His feeling of fraternity shaped his sympathetic portrayal of their violent natures and outrageous excesses. The bond of kinship he felt kept him from indulging in the kind of pained moralizing characteristic of so much of the Naturalist writing. He took more delight than umbrage at their excesses and refused to incur sentimental favor by growing maudlin over what their wild binges were doing to their wives and children and ultimately to society as a whole. *Le Baptême*, which treats the sailors' great appetite for alcohol, is a sympathetic apology for their behavior and appraisal of their lives: "When the bottle's full you see the reef, but when it's empty you don't" (XXI, 21).

Maupassant's own struggle with mental torment and artistic frustration paralleled those he was depicting in fiction. He too was struggling against superior forces; that is why he was so well able to depict the disappointment of strong men being brought to the harsh realization of their impending doom and defeat by their closeness to nature's violent manifestations. The sailor of *L'Ivrogne*, as filled with hatred as Baudelaire's hero of "Le Tonneau de la haine," murdered his wife in a stupor. Maupassant chose to show the act as the result of a primordial instinct and not to dwell upon its social implications. Characteristically, Maupassant was concerned here with man's—any man's—inability to cope with the forces that press in upon him and destroy him. It was the concern that made him continually assess his own life, and it was the concern that drove him to the conclusion that strong men and the petty clerks of Paris were all equally crushed. The pessimism that he generated in his twin studies of the strong and the weak and their equal defeat was initially inspired by Flaubert, but it grew through his own hard experience until it became distinct in its own right. The reader of Maupassant is well aware that his allowing the men of the waterfronts and the seas to be defeated means he sees no hope for any other group of the race.

V *Just One Sunday in a Week!*

The Seine meant life for the young man who could not have survived the insipid routine of the Ministries of the Marine or Education. Their futility was a debilitating insult to his creative purposes, and their dismal lack of motion was causing the death of his physical vigor. *Souvenir* contains the haunting reflection of a twenty-five-year-old, newly arrived in the city with its stifling Ministries: "before that bend, that villainous bend which once

rounded I have seen the end of the journey" (XXVII, 262). The
pain of his life in the early days in Paris was only allayed on Sundays when he was free to row on the Seine or to take a tour on
one of the boats for hire. The narrator's recollection in *Souvenir*
of the woman with the clod for a husband he had encountered on
the tour boat, *Hirondelle*, and had seduced before the day was
over was not likely pure fiction on Maupassant's part. Several
important autobiographical touches are evident in the story—
the name "Hirondelle" and memories of its use in *Madame
Bovary;* the presence of the cuckold and its relation to his work;
and most of all the proclivity of Maupassant to describe characters
with a neurotic fear of old age who found reminiscing upon their
youth both painful and exhilarating. The story appeared twelve
years after Maupassant had gone to Paris to work in the Ministry
of the Marine (1884). By that time he was free of the necessity
of earning his keep by an unimaginative servitude; he was by now
a successful writer. There is a nostalgic quality in the story when
its narrator complains of missing "the time when I had but one
Sunday a week," which more than anything else about the story
suggests by the analogous moods of author and fictional creation
that they are one and the same person. By 1884 Maupassant
seemed to sense that death was closing upon him rapidly. He
would have only nine more years, and of those only about seven
good ones. And so it seems certain that he looked back with a
yearning to recover those years of early literary struggle in Paris
when the hateful duties at the Ministry drained and distracted
him until he could not vilify them enough at the time. But now
he knew that they had been years of accomplishment and that
there would be none left to rival them in excitement and few
which would match their importance to his literary career. These
revelations emerging from the story make it less the recurring,
neurotic outburst against aging, and more profoundly a revelation
of the Maupassantian sadness. And too, it is evidence of how
inextricably Maupassant's happiness and brief optimism were
entwined with rowing, voyaging, sailing, and being with people
who in some way were associated with them.

The story *A Vendre* is another with obvious autobiographical
significance. The coastal setting for a place of residence was an
obsession with Maupassant. Here we have a character speaking
for Maupassant: "To set off on foot, at sunrise, and to walk in the

dew, along the fields, at the edge of the calm sea, what intoxication!" (XXI, 95). The walker becomes ecstatic at the sight of five boats loaded with singing people. Maupassant was ever capable of expressing joy at the sight of men and sea in harmony. The narrator's joy at this prospect throws him into a state of revery where there is no loneliness, no specter to terrify him. For Maupassant dreaming became a dangerous thing, a state that tended more and more to summon up the terrifying things that tormented his mind. But this story provides an example of the calming effect of the sea upon his imagination. And the narrator praises its efficacies in providing him with the insight that the wandering imagination is the only thing that can present to one a life that is always beautiful and golden. The optimism that is the result of this daydreaming is indeed the opposite mood from that which most often is the product of daydreaming in a Maupassantian story. The narrator finds the perfect cottage, and within, the portrait of its former mistress whose image for certain is the very ideal woman who has haunted his dreams but whom he had never hoped to find. He even learns that she left her husband, and this bit of information convinces him that she had fled only to await the time when she could return and share the house with him. "La Guillette" must have been just such a cottage, and Maupassant did on occasion entertain there the women he momentarily considered to be ideal, who too, for the most part were married women.

Le Havre with its exotic ships, bustling activity, sailors and dock hands, and its permanent citizens inspired some of Maupassant's best work. It taught him to understand profoundly the wretchedness of the man who embarks upon life's voyage with high hopes only to discover his unfitness for the journey and to end up in some small cranny of human misery, embittered and hopeless. This was the situation of a number of his stories, and Le Havre was the setting for them. It inspired character studies of those who only looked outward with a never-to-be-realized dream of some epic voyage, or of the return of their nonexistent ship of fortune. Rare is the story that reveals so moving an understanding of the pitiless gloom and despair of those who wait for an illusory happiness to come to them in the form of fortune instead of extracting what happiness there is out of struggling to obtain it, and of the shameful defeat and misery fate deals seem-

ingly indiscriminatingly to many who do set off in quest of
fortune as does *Mon Oncle Jules*. The story illustrates a sincerity
and mastery of control that do Maupassant great credit, and
one can feel that this is another of those stories that had grown
as much out of observation of real people and their tragic experience as out of the author's imagination. The young boy who tells
the story does not lose his faith in the sea as a symbol of hope in
spite of the knowledge that such hope has proven fatal in his
family. His mother has lost hope and become a vindictive shrew
whose pleasure consists of reviling her husband and generally
making life in the family unbearable. But the boy is still too
young to be willing to give up, and it is his optimism and faith
that overshadow the grim aspects of the story and make it
something more than a Realistic study. The port, the ship, the
tourists, all seen through his eyes, take on the exciting, adven-
turous, and heroic proportions that we seek in exotic subjects.
Maupassant understood the boy as well as he did the defeated
parents. For he had suffered for men he had seen fail in great
endeavors and live in exile because of their failure. He had hoped
a father would return to him, not for the fortune he would bring,
but just so he could point him out with pride to others. It is no
wonder that he knew how to comment upon how the little boy
looked forward to walking proudly at the side of his "heroic"
uncle. Joseph Devranche could not be a party to his family's
condemnation of the miserable oyster sheller, even though his
hopes had been betrayed like those of his creator. It is remarkable
that Maupassant's enthusiasm for the sea and seaports enables
him to create characters with the optimism of his own youth
long after he himself had become convinced that pessimism was
the only attitude the Realist should assume. He was still able to
turn back to the time when he thought he was suffering and
realize that the best days were those when he was complete
master of his time *only on Sundays.*

VI   *A Literary Sea Lion*

The sea seemed to inspire Maupassant's best critical thought.
His journal of random observations entitled *Sur l'Eau* contains
also some of his most honest self-criticism. The idea of literary
salons and their clever, arty banter could draw from him a range
of reactions, all unfavorable. And yet when on the water he wrote

candidly of his mania to be considered a literary lion—he would not have made such a confession to any of his associates in Paris. His sea voyaging purged him of this extravagant notion of his importance: "the lion [himself] soon forms a literary center, a church of which he is the god, the only god . . ." (XXVIII, 32). And why did he wish to be such a deity? Such a lion could have any woman he chose! One can speculate that the intrigue of *Fort comme la Mort,* and various incidents and characters in *Notre Coeur* were worked out when Maupassant was in this setting.

More important is the candor with which he views the making of a novel. The seascape seems to prepare his mind for thinking of problems which a busy, producing writer has little time for and yet which are basic to the quality of his style. He ponders, for example, the question of why he had turned from the *conte* to the novel when he had been doing so very well in the former and the latter had problems about it whose existence had been unknown to him. Maupassant's latter years were bitter ones for him, and not the least of the agitations that complicated his already precarious mental health was an increasing hostility against the criticisms of his novels. But here, on *Bel-Ami* alone save for François, he reached some very sane conclusions that provided an interesting justification for the venture. Besides what must be every shortstory writer's vague ambition to do something whose very bigness will still the tongue of their critics, he felt that novelists were more positive. He viewed them as the kind of goads society needed; they posed a threat to the complacent politicians and an imbecilic, uncritical populace because they peered into every corner, situation, and individual in search of material: "His eye is like a pump which absorbs everything, like a thief's hand always at work!" (XXVIII, 33). Maupassant revealed his intention of badgering society with his novels which by threatening to peer into all its facets would frighten it into respecting him and into turning its gaze thoughtfully upon its stupidity, pettiness, and mediocrity until it became sickened, as he had, of the image. He shows in this ambition his connection with the Naturalist cause; it is not often that he does so. Despite all of his protestations, what such avowals indicate is that Maupassant did need to know that he was reaching the people with his work. And moreover these admissions show that he had a rather naïve faith in his novels as the writings which would gather whatever acclaim there remained to be acquired.

How wrong he was! But his errors, often catastrophic, are as important in revealing Maupassant the man as are his sound judgments. Like a great many writers he was ineffective as a critic of his own work; he either overrated his accomplishments or underestimated his ability to achieve his ends within the limitations of the *conte*. The sea brought out these interior bouts whose brief recountings in *Sur l'Eau* give us a far better conception of his concerns as an artist. He talks frankly about his unhappiness with the thought in the then current literature. He tells of his ever-increasing dissatisfaction and boredom with reading; it was all the same. And this great displeasure led him to conclude that man's thought is immobile. Therefore he could reconcile the kind of idle dreaming he engaged in on his boat as the days raced by, rejoicing in the image of his boat floating senselessly in the void of the ocean as the earth floated in space and in the fact that these moments, these thoughts, belonged to him alone. "And I rejoice to perceive the emptiness of beliefs and vanity of hopes engendered by our flea-brained pride" (XXVIII, 45).

The great desire he had to be completely away from man and his "things" was realized in an effortless fashion for him because he had learned to love boats and the sea as a boy. It could be that the great emptiness, silence, and harmonious beauty of sea and sky had contributed a large share of his distaste for the crowded, noisy, and inharmonious ugliness that he saw in man's society. And if this was one of the things the sea did for him, then, it helped nurture and enlarge the pessimism that had been fired during his apprenticeship to Flaubert. Maupassant's pessimism is distinguishable from that of the master; it is not a copy, but a unique articulation of his sad truce with reality. The persistent pessimism of his stories on war, love, man's credulity, provincial life, and so on can be seen as the dominant tone of the thoughts that arose in him while he was floating only a few miles off the coast or making a long voyage. Likely Maupassant is persuasive enough to entice a reader to accept a conclusion he would rather not because of this sort of careful preparation by means of self-articulation. He found the silence of the sea at night the best place for such an exercise. The lone sounds of the boat's groanings told him "of what was happening, of what had fled, of what deceived, of what had disappeared, of what we will never attain" (XXVIII, 78).

VII   *The Sailor's Eye*

Maupassant's descriptions of the sea glint with an authenticity present only in the writings of those who have loved and struggled with the sea firsthand. There is the sailor's respect for omnipotence mingled with the adventuresomeness that makes him defy the odds. The writer whose navigating of the seas is left to others will see waves as waves. To Maupassant they were the sea's penning of its mood, and he deciphered their size, movement, rapid or slow, describing them in his writing because he was a sailor, not because he wished to be impressive:

Anyone who hasn't seen the open sea, that sea of mountains which move with rapid and weighty pace, separated by valleys which keep shifting from instant to instant, filled up and reformed ceaselessly, cannot divine, nor even suspect the mysterious, redoubtable, terrifying, and superb strength of the waves. (XXVIII, 164–65)

But if they were strong and ominous they were also gentle and soothing, capable of rocking away memories of landward avalanches and storms.

Even at sea, however, his thought takes a pessimistic turn. There was no escaping man, even there; and he often is reminiscent of Voltaire in the tone of his ironic musings:

Softly borne by the waters, the oars momentarily idle, far from land of which I can now see only its white crescent, I turn my thoughts to that wretched and petty humanity, to that wispy grain of life, so minuscule and tormented, which swarms upon this grain of sand, lost in the dust of a thousand worlds, to this miserable band of men, decimated by illnesses, crushed by avalanches, shaken and driven to frenzy by earthquakes, to those wretched little beings you can't see at a half kilometer's distance, yet are so vain and quarrelsome, who kill each other off when, as it is, they have only a little time allotted to them. (XXVIII, 188)

La Vie Errante evidences, as well, the calming influence of the sea in the life of Maupassant. A leisurely voyage upon it to some distant port of destination was the occasion for a deepening calmness toward the troubles that stormed with such persistence in his life. Just a day off the city of Cannes is described for its remarkable healing quality: "This tranquil day of floating about had cleansed my mind like a sponge wipe on a dirty pane; and a swarm of memories surged into my thoughts, memories of the world I had just left, of acquaintances, observed or loved" (III, 14). It provided a vantage point, then, from which he could view his difficulties with an efficacious resolve to solve them. And, like many an author, Maupassant needed to be remote physically from the regions, cities, and persons of which he wrote so that they might come into existence by the effort of his mind and hence possess a genuine artistic reality which is so far more meaningful than physical reality.

The voyage seemed to have stimulated his critical faculties in the field of literature. He argued convincingly, for example, for Baudelaire's right to occupy the position that critics much later reluctantly surrendered to him as a precursor of Symbolism. Baudelaire showed us what we must do with our senses. And Maupassant tries to imagine why it was that the obvious was so long in finding a genius to articulate it; if man had been created without ears the idea of music would be alien to him: "Yes, our organs are the nutrients and the masters of artistic genius. . . ." And he applied the lesson to his own ambitions as a novelist: "In general vision is dominant in the novelist" (III, 24). The doctrine, where it is applied in Maupassant's novels, is responsible for the several good ones. He did not, however, interest himself exclusively in relying upon the powers of well-trained senses, but instead ventured into the domain of the psychological novel under the influence of Paul Bourget, and in most cases it is regrettable.

VIII *The Sailor in Foreign Ports*

Maupassant's anger and pessimism in his journal seem to diminish as he enters a foreign port after a voyage of angry speculations. There is a sudden surge of the humanist in him. A seascape takes on an unaccustomed loveliness around a port city. The city itself, though, couldn't be uglier. It is the confrontation of purity and ugliness here that is most like their strange proximity in man. "If nothing is lovelier than the entrance to that port [Genoa] nothing is filthier than the entrance into the city itself" (III, 35–36). And yet the entrance into Genoa, mingled with his memory of the bourgeois ugliness of Paris as epitomized by the Eiffel Tower, and of that city's wealthy financiers and hucksters incapable of creating anything with beauty of form was a pleasant relief: Genoa was proof to him that despotic governments were at least capable of beauty.

Removed from France, he was able to express the political and social malaise of his time in terms of all the architectural ugliness it produced and to explain that the malady would not be cured by a generation without the slightest interest in beauty and taste.

His voyage to Sicily had perhaps the most profound effect upon his imagination of any of his travels. The catacombs, Wagner's hotel room, and especially the cloisters in which he found none of the harshness of northern cloisters impressed him: "The indecisive and poetic desire which forever haunts the human soul, which prowls about, maddening and inaccessible, seems just about to be realized" (III, 81). The eternal resting places of the gods, the temples, fascinated him for what was to him their silent testimony that there was no God, only greats among us, like us only in their mortality, whose immortality is their ideas.

Etna was the only hunk of land that could compare with the sea in power. It rose from the sea as if it had gained a standoff in the struggle between the land and the waves. And then, there was no theatrical backdrop to compare with that of the Taormina arena, nor was there a modern dramatist of great enough imagination to rise to the occasion of presenting a drama with the background of Etna and the sea: "those former men, those men of other times, had a soul and eyes which didn't resemble ours, and in their veins, with their blood, flowed something long gone: the love and admiration of Beauty" (III, 107).

The sea and voyaging brought out in Maupassant a humility which is rarely his forte. Here we see clearly a Maupassant filled with dissatisfaction with his work instead of one overly boastful. This is the real Maupassant, who, like his master, Flaubert, is tormented with his incapacity to do what he wants with words, descending into his very soul in search of a truly powerful novel he was never to find. He was in this climate a fine critic who recognized true greatness, and the prospect caused him to be discontented with himself. The masters were like the sea in their unique power to humble him. The sight of the Venus of Syracuse inspired him to the pronouncement of a remarkably clear statement of his theory of the ideal in art: "A work of art is superior only if it is, at once, a symbol and the exact expression of a reality" (III, 122). The artists of antiquity knew woman, with her qualities and faults, her female mind with its limitations and charms, and how to express the trouble a woman's presence can cause a man. Looking back to Maupassant's own masterful female types, one can surmise that his great philogynistic leanings were likely as much influenced by his travels and his admiring scrutiny of the art of antiquity as by his passion for setting the record straight regarding how his society held woman in check by a circle of prejudices and injustices.

The port of Venice provided Maupassant with a paradox. It was a place where trade, profit, and ambition, the sources of ugliness were paramount; and yet his praise of the beauty of Venice is lavish. The men who visit Venice do not lie about what they have seen, for "we look at it with our dreams." The truth is in the imagination of the dreamer, and "they see with their imagination much more than with their eyes" (III, 245–46). What better city could there be for Maupassant than one which uses the sea for its streets? His description of a gondola ride shows that sound knowledge of the poetry of boats and waters that is characteristic of Maupassant's life: "one is caressed by the movement, caressed in mind and body, penetrated by a sudden and continuous physical enjoyment and by a profound feeling of spiritual well-being" (III, 248).

But a voyage across the bay to visit Vesuvius aboard a Neapolitan vessel draws a complaint from the disciplined sailor. The filth aboard the vessel is obnoxious to him and spoils the experience.

By and large, however, port cities are the most exciting for Maupassant. His enthusiasm lends to his meticulous observation of their way of life a vitality and authority rare among writers on the subject. He has that knack of using brilliant and poetic descriptions without draining the life from his narrative as is so often the case among writers. This manner of giving to his setting a certain vibrancy all its own and yet so much a part of the tale is an extra bonus in his writing. At one time Maupassant gave serious consideration to writing a series describing the French port cities. It would have been an excellent series, or as he says, a "charming book."

IX   *The Sea and the Novels*

The sea is most active in several of Maupassant's novels. When one recalls the autobiographical aspect of *Une Vie*, he cannot help but reflect upon how the importance of the sea in the novel completes it. It is not strange to see the sea having its effect upon the characters of the novel, especially remembering whom the characters were very likely patterned after. The intensity of the influences is what strikes one most. Clearly it is the sway of the sea upon the author's own life that is here being recounted. The frequency with which a character will emotionalize over a scene dominated by the sea; the strange omnipotent quality it possesses to attract man's admiration and activities and to toy with his aspirations; the manner in which its limitless moving desolation can somehow restore a soul bruised by finitude; and its final and inevitable triumph—all of these Maupassantian attitudes are present in the work. Sometimes we see them in such a way as to enhance all of our prior glimpses of them. In this area as in that of the Maupassant family relationship, *Une Vie* proves to be a storehouse of some of Maupassant's most private reflections, a must for the perceptive biographer whose task it is to see the real man amidst the latter's efforts to fictionalize. There is a distinct impression that when he speaks of the sea in *Une Vie* there is no exaggeration. But such a conclusion is cloudy at best for the reader not familiar with Maupassant's life.

The young heroine, Jeanne, like her creator, yearns to get out of her cloistered school and back into the life of the Normandy coast. Clearly, her happy reaction and her mind's-eye impressions of Normandy give Maupassant the chance to indulge himself in expressing the pleasureful side of his native region. Rarely does one see him more enthusiastic. But when one knows that all of this exuberant enthusiasm for life is but an ironic prelude to Jeanne's bitter disenchantment with it, he realizes how very close to the author's own situation is that of his heroine. The book provides, then, what might be termed vibrant and haunting

memories of Maupassant. As yet we do not see the sick and
harassed man for whom the sea became a last refuge, an escape
from the land with its people.

Jeanne, strong like the youthful Maupassant, swam out of sight
of shore, living to the fullest the precious moments of freedom.
She sailed with her father, who liked the company of the fisher-
men. The Baron, caught by Maupassant recalling fishing expedi-
tions, is a portrait that surely would serve for one of the author
himself:

He loved to hear the mast creaking, to breathe in the hissing and cool
night gusts; and after tacking about for a long while in order to relocate
the buoys, the top of a steeple and the lighthouse of Fécamp, while
picking his way around a crest, he enjoyed being completely immobile
under the first flares of the rising sun which made the gummy backs of
wide fan-shaped skates and the gray stomachs of fat flounder glisten on
the decks. (II, 30)

This was to Maupassant the real life for which men were destined,
the life which gave him the brief happy period of his life.

The importance of the port of Etretat to Maupassant's life is
better understood by its presentation in his fiction. Any biographer
will note whenever a writer refers to his native town or region. It
is most rare, however, to find a writer for whom his town meant
so much. Maupassant presents it from so many different points
of view that the one patient enough and interested enough to
read the whole of his work will discover that his understanding
of it is truly extraordinary, for at no time does a character, whatever his type and talent, present the scene through eyes that are
not truly his own. And very often we do become aware that a
character is not really seeing the thing as he would if he were
really what the author represents him to be. Not so in Maupassant.
And this is one of the great assets of his work. Here is what is
seen by the sailor looking at the town as it looms up in the distance: "Over there, astern, brown sails broke from the white jetty
of Fécamp, and yonder, off the bow, a strangely formed rock,
rounded and pierced with sunlight, resembled closely the face of
an elephant sinking its trunk into the waves. It was the little port
of Etretat" (II, 46).

The role of the sea emerges at the beginning of the long novel: it is on a sailing trip that Jeanne first experiences a vague tenderness for the husband who will ruin her, Julien. Maupassant has many of his characters make the decisions that will make or break their happiness upon or beside the sea. And as we have shown, a great many of the favorable and unfavorable turns in the course of his own life were resultant to decisions arrived at at sea. But such a moment and setting as the author describes in the following lines lends itself so completely to a person's sentiments that his making some sort of move is almost inevitable: "The sun climbed as if to consider from a greater height the vast sea spread beneath it; but the latter, as if suddenly becoming coquettish, enveloped itself in a light fog which veiled it from the rays" (*ibid*). If the ability to use meaningful metaphors and symbols is truly the mark of genius, then Maupassant clearly belongs in distinguished company. What Maupassant sought from sailing, from voyaging is continually upon Jeanne's lips: "how very well off one is when one dreams, completely alone" (II, 52). And her honeymoon voyage takes her to the very places Maupassant speaks of so enthusiastically in *La Vie Errante*, Greece, Italy, and Corsica. She had rebelled at her husband's choice of Switzerland.

Early stripped of her illusions about her husband, Julien, it is to the sea that Jeanne turns with the prospect of doing away with herself. A pang about what her death would do to her mother caused her to vacillate in answering the sea's call for the instant required for friends to grab her and draw Jeanne back from the cliff's edge. Because she loved sailing, it was quite natural for her to attempt to buy her errant son back with a boat. (The incident is reminiscent of Maupassant's letters to his mother describing his ambitions to have a boat of his own when he returned home from school.) The lure of a boat would have brought Maupassant running. But not so Paul, his fictional creation. Paul accepted the boat but only as a means to escape from her. Later, ironically, he bled her of money in order to enter into a steamship venture. In the end, the thought of living too far away from the sea to be able to visit it upon whim is sadder for her than anything she has endured. Her farewell is written with a loving pathos: "then she went out to bid adieu to the sea. It was near the end of September, a lowered gray sky seemed to weigh upon the world; the saddish, yellowish waves stretched out of sight" (II, 333). Not being able to see the sea is a hell for her:

"Oh! how I'd love to see the sea!" The thing that she missed so strongly was the sea, her great neighbor for twenty-five years, the sea with its salty air, its anger, its scolding voice, its powerful swells, the sea that each morning *she used to see from the window at "des Peuples,"* that she breathed in day and night, that she felt near her, that she had begun to love like another person, never regarding it as anything else. (italics mine) (II, 342–43)

Her strange hallucination on the occasion of a return to visit her old home suggests the same pattern of mental aberration that haunted Maupassant during his last days: "she thought she saw— she really saw, as she had so often seen, her father and her mother warming their feet by the fire" (II, 374). Her return to her home by the sea had momentarily given her a glimpse of the old happiness.

X   *The Eyes of the Port*

Maupassant had the kind of imagination capable of making his nostrils flare with the "harsh and good odor of the coast" whenever he was far from it. He never wished to forget the smell. But his attitude toward one necessary feature of the harbor was ambivalent. He often wished to forget the beacon lights. Doubtless his sometime aversion to them was caused by the ironic symbolism which his imagination gave to them. Metaphorically they probe his conscience and the consciences of his characters like the eye of God. And in this capacity they often illuminate briefly shapes he would rather not see. They bring into the mind but bits and pieces of a totality that the imagination often works into monstrous patterns. And then there was to him the irony of its role as a beacon: "One of them especially irritated me. They went out every thirty seconds to come on again at once; it was indeed an eye, that one, with its lid ceaselessly lowered over its fiery stare" (*Les Epaves,* I, 88). We see what an impression watching the harbor beacons made upon Maupassant by finding that he alludes to them not only here but in a key passage of *Pierre et Jean.* The exquisite artistry of this novel is evident in its restrained but powerful symbolical and ironic passages among which one of the finest, as we shall see, deals with the harbor lights.

The sea is the great pulling force in *Pierre et Jean*. It brought Père Roland to Le Havre; it drew forth the competition between the two brothers for the attentions of Madame Rosémilly which Jean won handily; it drew forth from Pierre's imagination the co-minglings of jealousy and fact responsible for his penetrating the truth about him and his younger "brother"; and it drew Pierre away from his mother at the end of the novel in a magnificently symbolic scene. And yet its omnipotence toward the Roland family was in direct parallel to its sway upon the creator of the novel. Nowhere do Maupassant's feelings of awe and enthusiasm for the sea transform themselves into clearer literary expression than in this novel. The sea metes out to the characters the things which they crave along with the evil harvest of their cravings. It is fate itself. That is the sea that Maupassant knew, loved, and feared.

The symbol of old Roland, staring with all of the blind concentration of his meagre soul upon the sea, scouting for a ship is magnificent. What a symbol for the kind of bourgeois mediocrity that had drawn the wrath of Maupassant's master, Flaubert, in *Bouvard et Pécuchet!* Always looking out where he should not be concentrating, the old man is foolishly, not tragically, blind to the evidences about him! And Pierre, already the victim of a cruel imagination, staring out to sea at night and learning the very things he has sought to discover with the horror of a man discovering he has cancer.

Maupassant liked the sea's honesty. It did not hedge. As a sailor he knew that one does not do battle with the sea to win, that there is no question of man's ability to contend with the sea on equal terms. But he had great respect for those with the courage to enter into the struggle. He found answers by wrestling with it, as did his hero, Pierre. And no matter how great the odds against him, Maupassant preferred this natural habitat to the neurotic society man had created for himself where dishonesty and pusillanimity were the rule. Any biographer who fails to understand Maupassant's close attachment for the sea will fail in his efforts to make meaningful critical remarks about many of his works, and in particular *Pierre et Jean*.

Maupassant knew that he was only an amateur seaman. The knowledge made him more convincing in his description of

Monsieur Roland, whose lack of even an amateurish knowledge of sailing accentuates the absurd distance between the man's dreams and reality, a major cause for his downfall. A writer with the same superficial nautical knowledge of a character whom he endowed with exorbitant maritime aspirations would have been far less successful in making his reader aware of the tragic discrepancy which is a key in this novel. Maupassant's boyhood sailing taught him what the real thing was: he understood that the sea offered a real solace, a meaningful escape from the tedium of a land-locked existence, but only in direct proportion to one's capacity to engage it in struggle. The fact that the tide does not bring in what so many of Maupassant's characters such as Roland wait upon becomes the inevitable result of their hoping that by admiring a great god he will somehow appear miraculously to answer their supplications. People who dream great dreams without either the willingness or indeed the capacity for achieving them are always destroyed by Maupassant. It is interesting to note this important manifestation of the theme of "Bovarysme" in his work. In allowing Roland to go on believing that his life by the sea has made up for all of those weary shopkeeping hours of Paris, that his move here where he can rest his eyes upon the sea has solved the problem of happiness for him, Maupassant is extremely kind, although for many the oblivion to cuckoldry in which he allows old Roland to remain is cruel proof of the determinism that relentlessly condemns a stupid man to stupidity.

The evidence of how Maupassant brooded upon the ports and their surroundings again comes to the fore as Pierre becomes hypnotized by the winkings of the lighthouses in the harbor of Le Havre. As he watches them probing the darkness, he too begins to probe the mystery of his brother's good fortune in receiving such a generous inheritance. Metaphorically speaking, the lighthouses light Pierre's way until he emerges with the fact that his mother had been an adulteress, an illumination which he had sought without really wishing to be blinded by its light. The exquisite study of the mind, troubled by vague, unarticulated suspicions represented by this passage of the novel does credit to the greatest of the psychological novelists. The beacons sweep across the water, and in their rapid circle cast such momentary illumination upon objects as to leave the viewer uncertain as to what he has seen. In the same way, moments of dazzling brilliance are followed by obscurity in the mind of Pierre so that he does not know what he has seen. Maupassant the sailor had experienced moments when upon the entrance into a harbor the beacon lights had illuminated shapes which, the instant they were again plunged into darkness, stimulated his imaginative suspicions and led him into errors of judgment. There is no scene in Maupassant whose metaphorical authenticity is more outstanding than this one because Maupassant knew what it was for the sailor to grope his way through the night, and he knew the mistakes that such groping fostered: "opening and closing like eyes, the eyes of ports, yellow, red, green, watching over the dark sea covered with ships . . ." (XI, 42–43). With this passage Maupassant seizes our awareness with the kind of tenacious grasp that is in the highest tradition of the prose raconteur. The comparison between the thoughts and suspicions of a troubled man and those of the sailor who relies upon beacons to aid his navigation is one of those poetic bonuses that we hope for but seldom find in the work of a novelist.

XI   *The Voices of the Port*

"Nearing the port area he heard coming from the open sea a sinister and lamentable cry, like the lowing of a bull, but more consistent and more powerful. It was the siren's cry, the distress call of ships lost in the fog" (XI, 43). Maupassant saw the ship lost in a fog as the metaphor for the malady which beset Pierre. It is ironic that the metaphor is also applicable to the last days of the author's own life. The same thing happened to him that happened to his hero, Pierre: friend was transformed into foe by his unrelenting notion that everyone was against him. Maupassant at the last of his life harkened unto the call of his suspicions just as did Pierre. He became unreasonable in interpreting the sounds he heard. The sighs and laughter of lovers on the beach led Pierre to wonder if these weren't the sounds of those who with joyous abandon were crushing someone else. Maupassant also grew to hate the scene of that vast beach which "was but a love market where some sold themselves, others gave themselves" (XI, 124). And this from a man who had once prided himself in being a Don Juan!

But that he turns upon the sea, that he reveals the petty soul of the bigot whom he ordinarily despised, will more distress than surprise an admirer of Maupassant. That he allows his hero, Pierre, to be the defector should not confuse us: Pierre contributes much to the biography of Maupassant, and if we do not understand the imaginative creation we will miss much that is significant about the creator. It is grievous to see how suspicion works upon the mind of Pierre, because it recalls how the anguish of doubt and pessimism Maupassant experienced contributed to the disintegration of his faculties. Disease was not the only thing responsible for the author's rapid deterioration, nor was it the lone cause of his foolish suspicions that he was being robbed, cheated, and victimized by the very people who were interested in him and in what he had given to the world—there was this cynicism, this pessimism regarding the integrity of the human race that made an old man of him before his time.

Pierre's agony is the product of his loss of faith in his mother's integrity. To have hung all his hopes of proving the nobility of the race upon his personal idea that his mother would prove to be a symbol of honor and purity was a mistake of sufficient magnitude to assure him of a life of disillusionment and suffering. His mistake, though, is characteristic of man with his narrow perceptions: it is this that accounts for Pierre's appeal for us. Seeing his miscalculation as a universal truth strengthens one's assurance that Maupassant was exploring psychological states familiar to him in the presentation of his character. Pierre's extreme sensitivity which causes him to behave with the irrationality of a mad animal is not unlike the sensitivity that caused Maupassant to behave sometimes in a deranged manner. *Perhaps* when Maupassant tells us that Pierre frightened his mother with his determination to get the facts on what kind of woman she had been, he is not recounting a scene that passed between himself and his own mother. Laure de Maupassant was doubtless at times afraid of her son, though she had nothing to hide from him. Pierre's mother was like Laure; she found it impossible to hold his intemperate outbursts against him. The image of Pierre, alone, that "other one," is familiar to the one who follows the biography of Maupassant. The strength of the sea, its vastness, its turmoil, is shown to resemble that of the mind of the hero,

Pierre. What better image is there than this to suggest the struggle within Maupassant's soul?

XII *No Home on Land*

Jean's greatest talent is for rapid solutions which serve his interests. He is the one who discovers that there is a position for a physician aboard an ocean liner. It is his gilded description of such a life and its possibilities that sells everyone else on the idea that they should not feel guilty at getting rid of Pierre, that what they are really interested in is finding for him the good life. It is Pierre's mother who expresses the sense of hurt and alienation that Maupassant knew during the years of declining health, after he had lost the man he had wanted for a father: "Life is villainous! If you once find a bit of sweetness in it, you become guilty of abandoning yourself to that sweetness and pay very dearly for it in later years" (XI, 208). Madame Roland seems to have known more about the famous writer than his own mother: doubtless Maupassant has her express what he would have liked for his mother to articulate.

It is important to note that Pierre suffered because he had no home upon the land. Maupassant seems never to have been hurt by whatever was denied him in the way of family life. But this lack in Pierre's life being highlighted makes one wonder if Maupassant's seeming indifference to the ordinary conceptions of family unity is not a myth which he created in order to assure himself that his ideas of family relationships were as remote and superior to the bourgeois conceptions as those of a god. His description of Pierre's emotions concerning the prospect of a life upon the sea is most revealing: "the bewilderment of a beast without shelter, a material anguish at being a wanderer who has no roof and that the rain, wind, storm, all the world's brutal forces are going to assail" (XI, 221–22). Significant is the fact that Pierre sees his life of the wandering pariah as the product of his mother's behavior which he refuses to condemn before the entire family whom he feels incapable of understanding.

The sea has its negative as well as its positive effect throughout the novel. Nowhere is its dual effect more evident than in the end. The sea will give Pierre a new home, will provide the family with a means of ridding itself of the one who knew things that would have destroyed it. The man responsible for his wife's adultery is the only member of the family unaware of why Pierre has to leave. The consistency that marks the bourgeois class, proud of its unwavering moral attitudes, is nowhere more sharply satirized by Maupassant than in his presentation of Monsieur Roland repeating the action which had identified him at the beginning of the novel: here again he is enthusing over the dimensions and destination of the great ship upon which Pierre is departing. And this at the same time the rest of the family is at least aware of the solemnity of parting! Maupassant shows us a reason for not envying the unruffled happiness of the mediocre. How the others in his family must suffer because of his insensitivity! All he sees is the great ship passing, and not the bewildered, pleading arms of his wife outstretched toward the parting vessel. Maupassant's bitterness toward the father is never more in evidence.

Here as everywhere in Maupassant the sea is the final solace, the last challenge, the horizon which offers much but also demands much. Only writers who have been as much under its influence as was Maupassant can deliver more than platitudes describing how it plays the role of God in the lives of certain men. Such a role it had in the life of Maupassant. Shorn of its influence, Maupassant's life and work indeed would have been of far less importance for us.

CHAPTER 5

Maupassant and the War

I *When Death Once Enters*

MAUPASSANT'S life drifted literally and figuratively upon the tides of war and peace. We have viewed one aspect of his portrayal of the war of 1870 in our discussion of the women who influenced his life and art. Now let us move from the restrictive purpose of showing how Maupassant always sought and found superior qualities in his women characters to a consideration of what were his attitudes on war. Realizing that his work would not have been nearly so inspired were wars a thing of the past, he nonetheless gave the indication that he would have preferred to live in a world where man spared himself their agonies. Maupassant's reactions to war are more ambiguous and paradoxical than those of the twentieth-century French writers who have had so much influence in shaping our attitudes on the subject. War was a grim business to him: but it would be a mistake to see moral objections as the lone specters that haunted and tormented him; rather one must face the fact that, in the beginning, Maupassant hated the specter of defeat more vehemently than any other of war's ghosts. If one needs to verify this conclusion he has but to recall how many stories of Maupassant relate how an individual reacted against the conqueror in such a way as to show that it was not the conquered, but the conqueror who has been defeated. Later works, as we shall see, present quite another aspect of war.

Judging from Maupassant's work, defeat weighed heavily upon his life. His characters smolder in silent shame or wrench themselves free of the tyrant's grasp by an act of defiance that would be labeled as either a foolish gesture or the product of madness by the more reasoning, philosophizing members of the society. Maupassant was angered that it required a sort of "madness" to

go against the "best interests" of the people by refusing to be
dominated by the conqueror. Madness or humiliation—Maupassant chose to praise those whose acts were condemned as madness. In *La Folle* we see a Maupassant almost despising his fellow
countrymen whom conquest had not driven to madness. "Formerly, at twenty-five, she had lost, in a single month, her father,
her husband, and her newborn babe. When death once enters a
house, it comes back nearly always immediately, as if it knew
the door" (VII, 37). Rare is the metaphor in Maupassant more
moving and more significant in revealing his personal attitude
than the one above. Maupassant saw war as a death-dealer, not
simply because combatants were killed by it, but because it
killed the spirit of people. The only heroic individuals for him
in the France of the 1870's were those who were "unreasonable"
enough or "mad" enough to refuse to be conquered. War indeed
took its toll. More there were who preferred to "get along," to
"rebuild," to "face facts" than there were who would defy the
enemy. Maupassant believed the real enemy was silence, the
attitude that "nothing can be done"; and although he never took
on the invader in direct confrontation, he accomplished much in
showing that a steadfast conventional silence, if it is dignified, is
ineffectual as a means of turning back an enemy bent upon shaping you to fit his mold. The way people fell into acceptance after
the Franco-Prussian debacle must have inspired his determined
attack upon the thoughtless manner in which people capitulate
to the conventional opinions and standards. Without the war he
might never have become concerned with the histories of those
rare individuals who challenge and who question before they
accept. Indeed, he might not have spoken out so forcefully
against the uncritical acceptance by the people of social and
moral conventions which, he felt, kept the hypocritical and the
irresponsible in power. If the various challenges to the accepted
made by his imaginative creations did not by themselves succeed
in turning things around, they did give the necessary courage to
the timid and the weak to pose the challenging questions. Maupassant, himself, did a great deal, despite the seeming unsuccess
of his attack upon convention, to dispel the fear that paralyzes
both the speech and action of persons who remain in ineffectual
silence.

He despised the time, effort, and human life that governments expend in staying prepared to make war. And yet, he suffered deeply from the ineffective, asinine charges made by his country-men at the wrong time and in the wrong place, their disorderly retreats, the fouled-up battle plans, and especially the inept and pompous officers who contributed to the defeat. He was torn between the crime of preparing for war and the feeling that being unprepared was just as great a crime. He sympathized with sol-diers caught in the dreadful monotony of army life; he was all too familiar personally with its grim emptiness. His descriptions of this aspect of war have the especial poetic poignancy of a man whose physical vigor caused him to rebel against the dusty, plodding life of the bureaucrat and to regard war as an arena where action and heroism were the norm. But there too, alas, there was only boredom. The following describes the life of hated Prussian soldiers; but it expresses, nevertheless, the frus-tration of all soldiers and the bitter disappointment of the indi-vidual who seeks in army life an outlet for his frustrated energies: "A fog of acrid smoke drowned them, and they appeared to be sinking into a lethargic and sad drunken stupor, in that dismal debauch of those who have nothing to do" (X, 8).

How well he was able to depict the wretched and inefficacious counterfeits a defeated people offer themselves as a balm to their consciences crying out for heroic deeds! He knew these little people and felt drawn to them as fellow sufferers in defeat. But only in war does he depict them with such patience: in other situations they are more often than not repugnant to him. A village priest redeems himself momentarily in the mind's eye of Maupassant when he refuses to ring the bell of the village church as ordered by the conquerors. It is a small and ineffectual rebel-lion, but to Maupassant it has enough significance to cause him to hesitate before making blanket condemnations of priests in his writings. This kinder treatment he extended to the French villager in general. Though many stories decry the mediocrity and hypocrisy of the villager, those in which the war or the oc-cupation are factors reveal an unusual Maupassantian tolerance of the peasant mentality.

The treatment of the two fishing companions in *Deux Amis* provides us with evidence of the war's effect in transforming Maupassant's usually pessimistic attitude toward his contem-poraries. The characters in question are loafers who haven't the slightest interest in being of service to anyone or any cause but themselves. They represent distinctly that class referred to as "shiftless humanity." They are reminiscent in their worthlessness and dullness of so many of the subjects who inspired Flaubert to draw them as the meanest sort of mediocrity capable of following any directive or supporting any cause indiscriminately. They are a part of that menacing tide of humanity which the master taught his pupil to be pessimistic about. Maupassant saw their patient complacency as capable of engulfing whatever good there was in the world. He could not see it as a sort of salvation. But in this story we find his usual cynicism shaken to the point of bestowing upon his heroes a certain philosophical dignity: their assessment that it is man's stupidity alone that causes him to kill his neighbor coincides with Maupassant's own (X, 216). Their refusal to turn over the fish to the Prussians in exchange for their lives, moreover, reveals resolve and dignity worthy of the greatest philosophers. To the Prussian officer it seems but another stupid sacrifice to self-respect; but to a people humiliated, any stand against the enemy, be it small or ridiculous, aids in the restoration of the pride and dignity of all the conquered and thereby becomes a sign of an eventual deliverance. His own personal suffering over the defeat not only inspired his stories but caused him to seek out some admirable, redeeming qualities in his compatriots. It is seldom that we see him casting aside his cynicism regarding the people. But the defeat seems to have, temporarily at least, inspired a certain optimistic view of the people. If it did not convince him to abandon his pessimism, it did lessen the bitterness which so often characterized his pronouncements on the people. Nevertheless, even when writing about the war Maupassant was stingy with his optimism concerning his compatriots. The hero of *Un Duel* stands up to the enemy out of season: he should have fought so furiously against the invader when there had still been a chance that his fighting might have helped drive him off. Now, owing more to luck than to skill, he kills a Prussian braggart in a duel. But he is little better than his opponent; for it is the personal vanity born of wealth that inspires his late and meaningless revolt. Maupassant's ironic recounting of the incident reveals the severe pessimism regarding his fellow countrymen and their motivations that is the dominant note in his writing.

II *War and the Transformation of an Attitude*

Maupassant's ambivalence regarding the female has often been discussed. We have seen how he admired her courage and resolve during the cruel years of the occupation. His male-ego-oriented scorn for woman could not hold up against the repeated examples of her enlightened and effective struggle against the darkness of defeat to which he was a witness and about which he wrote some of his finest stories. Much has already been said regarding the women of these stories, but it is certainly pertinent to emphasize here how different his entire notion of womanhood would have been had there been no war; for it was clearly the war that unwarped his prejudice. Never would be have viewed her as a creature with courage and resolve above that of the male had he not been forced to by the various dramas played out before him during the struggle. He would have preferred, in fact, to cling to the more conventional conceptions of her. Had he done so, his work would have been vastly different. The women would have remained the amusing, the gullible or sly, the bitchy or sweet creatures of the fabliaux tradition which so strongly influenced him.

His observance of women in war made him acutely aware of the danger of being so strong a raconteur as to forget that people in stories must be real—not mere types—if the story is to be great. Thus, he gave more attention to the art of inventing situations where a character's rise or fall was dependent upon choices and interpretations, and not upon a vague fate—in short, their movements upward or downward have a finished reality. Many of Maupassant's creations might have forever lamely mimicked *real* people but for the war and its stimulation of his curiosity regarding the behavior of the female half of the race. His women are real in spite of the fact that they behave in a manner that suggests their superiority to those whom we have come to view as "real." It became increasingly difficult for Maupassant's contemporaries to avoid reassessing their female prejudice—these were real women, not mythical types whose power was more fancy than fact. Detractors, male chauvinists, and men generally would have liked to dismiss his women. His attack upon the myth about war's being the stuff of muscle and male heroics was unrelenting. To assault such a myth was to betray honored con-

ventions of his time. That his first real chance to attack the anti-
feminist conventions of his time should be injurious to his career,
which depended upon a favorable male acceptance, was clear to
him. But once committed, he never gave up or turned back on
his own personal convictions about her. Perhaps the war's greatest impress upon Maupassant was not, after all, his awareness
of defeat frustration and futility, but its crushing of the old one-
sided, misogynistic attitude that had dominated his thinking.

III   *The War and the* Beau Geste

Maupassant was very much aware of war's horrible mutila-
tions. He did not like the kind of writing that uses an unfortunate victim's physical affliction as an excuse to promote a vulgar
sentimentality. To present a critique of such efforts he dreams
up a tearful reunion for the amputee of *L'Infirme,* a traveling
companion across from whom he finds himself seated on a certain
journey. He concocts, in much the same way as the writer in
search of the praise of the vulgar, a sentimental fantasy about
who the man is, why he is carrying toys and candy, and what
will be the scene on the station platform when he arrives at his
destination. It is all quite absurd, but it provides the kind of
story that is more up for sale than anything else. For, the man
was *not* returning to his family. There was *no* wife to be brave
and loving despite the affliction. Instead, the man had refused
to marry the woman he loved and who loved him quite as much
after as before his misfortune; indeed, he had forced her to
marry another. He had insisted on severing himself, just as his
feet had been severed from his body, from all the significance of
the multiple possibilities and experiences of a life after a tragic
dismemberment. All but the experience of masochism. It is to
rekindle this tragic emotion that he so often comes to visit his
"nephews," "nieces," and their parents.

The story has a sad parallel in Maupassant's own life. He himself was not so far removed from sharing sentiments similar to
those of his hero: he too came to feel he had given up for his
art the wife who could have been the needed companion against
the haunting fears that beset him at night during his later life.
A strain of personal masochism gave Maupassant his touching
understanding of the strange amputee: his early struggle to sub-

limate his physical vigor for the sake of art, then the doomed efforts to cope with the disease which impaired not only body but mind, and finally his loneliness, a self-imposed exile with all of the masochistic connotations evident in the aforementioned story. In a strange way the tale reflects his mounting conviction from the mid-1880s onward that he was a martyr, misunderstood and hence necessarily estranged. This exaggerated view of his personal suffering seems to have been flagellated by his perceptions of war's martyrdoms. The strong interest in masochism and his genuine sympathy for it in his fellow creatures came from his personal conviction that he had given his best, his manhood and his love, for a race of indifferents. Maupassant's life expresses an ever-widening alienation. He clearly enjoyed the pain it caused him, however, and just as did the hero of *L'Infirme*, he took every opportunity to intensify its agony.

Of further interest is Maupassant's sympathy for the male hero. *L'Infirme* is a war story where the male is, in Maupassant's eyes, at least, more heroic than the female. The fact is that he was fictionalizing a psychological state strongly resembling his own. In *Boule de Suif*, *Le Lit 29*, and other works, extrospection is the method of viewing his male characters; and what we see condemns them. But here he uses introspection which becomes more credible and seems even more revealing once the implication is made that the untrue story was the direct consequence of extrospection. It is an involved technique. The story makes one aware of the difference in the males whom Maupassant causes to act and those whose drama is more a psychological one: the former fare badly, the latter usually much better—for example, *Pierre et Jean*, Pierre the hero of *Monsieur Parent*, and numerous other male characters.

IV *Disillusionment*

Maupassant's romantic preconception of war as a testing ground was too optimistic. His assessment of the male species as weak became a fixed notion: man had shown himself to be, in Maupassant's mind, unwilling even to enter upon the testing ground with any purpose but surrender. It was a sad disillusionment for him to decide that his worst suspicions about man's pusillanimity were confirmed. Quite naturally, then, he turned his attention to the other half of the race. And what he saw was woman with a capacity to live amidst the defeats man had created for himself, not only live with them, but turn them into a victory for herself.

His disillusionment took another turn. Because his notions of war had been largely what they are for one who has gleaned them from the storybooks with their aristocratic orientation, he was unprepared for the bestiality that is so large a part of it— the side that is seen only after one has purged himself of all of the deluding battle hymns and come to a consideration of the real thing. He grew up suddenly, as so many are forced to do. His eyes were opened. The result is that he peered into its most revolting aspect in stories such as *Tombouctou* in an effort to shock others into an awareness of the need for a critical examination of war as a disease caused by man. Denouncing war became the theme here, as it did in his highly revelatory discussion of the various problems of his world and art in *Sur l'Eau,* about which much has already been said. *Tombouctou* is especially interesting because of the author's choice of theme: he begins in a tone that deludes the reader into the impression that the writer knows he is exaggerating and intends also that the reader know it; but then, suddenly, it becomes clear that the tone is far from hyperbolic and that the events are real. One is forced to accept the war as without a single redeeming feature. Nothing, no consideration, be it political or a question of honor, could possibly justify the terrible consequences of war's effect upon those who fight it; for war is so constituted as to strip man completely of his humanity. Cannibalism is but the ultimate symbol in Maupassant's art of the essence of war. Those who foster wars and those who fight them are no longer human in his eyes.

Not content to let the reader off the hook with a mere presentation of the symbol of cannibalism, Maupassant has the officer-narrator represent those who read and are "concerned" but who end up doing nothing. For, even when he realizes the source of the meat Tombouctou keeps bringing in, he still jealously guards that civilized repugnance for accepting the analogy that Maupassant wishes to force upon him and upon us all, *that men eating the flesh of their brothers is what war is,* and that it really doesn't make any difference, so far as the extent of guilt is concerned, whether you ever literally masticate a piece of human flesh or not. The officer's skin still crawls like that of a "civilized" European at the thought, though he and his civilization have never cringed at the thought of centuries of killing and figuratively cannibalizing their neighbors.

It was, then, not Maupassant's fondness for the horrible, though it was great, that inspired the irony and symbol of *Tombouctou*. The story reflects how the war ultimately changed Maupassant's life view. At first he had been like his fellow countrymen: the sudden capitulation of his country had shocked him into seeking about for a place to put the blame, into a desperate search for examples of nobility and courage in defeat. But unlike his fellow countrymen, he had soon found himself incapable of ignoring the fact that defeat was but a small part of war, no matter how tragic, and that it behooved the writer and thoughtful person to denounce war solely upon grounds of its immorality. He knew that it was easy for the defeated to decry war; for momentarily the defeat of France had lent drama and eloquence to his outcries against it. But what if France had been the victor? War was still war, still just as immoral, no matter which side of the fence one occupied. *Tombouctou* is a small tributary from the dominant stream of his treatment of the defeated in war; but the tributary comes more and more to resemble a great river as we pursue it toward the end of his writing. The story is a very strong repudiation of war as inhuman, as immoral, and hence as unworthy of man. Here and elsewhere, his probing of the moral question regarding war suggests how he is related to Voltaire on the one hand and to the twentieth-century writers in France on the other.

He was cynical about the efficaciousness of his repudiation of war. The cynicism robs his work of the vigor that some modern attacks upon wars possess. There is none of the quixotic hope to lend an attractiveness to his condemnation. And hence he is little known for his contribution to the literature on the theme. Maupassant felt that his denunciations of war would do no more to arouse the people to revolt than had his assault upon the conventions which held woman back from competing equally with the male. He viewed the possibility that man would change with the deepest pessimism. But he was not a hardened cynic; he wished he could enjoy the cynic's release at the very certainty of man's unchangeability. But he experienced none of the satisfactions of cynicism. "Happy are those who do not experience an immense loathing at the certainty that nothing passes and that everything fatigues" (XXVIII, 41). If we look at his life, though, we can see why it was that he did not enjoy even that small particle of satisfaction that cynicism can give: nothing changed for the better for him; his father did not mend his ways and transform himself into Maupassant's ideal father; his brother grew more and more of a burden; and the oppression of his mother, in spite of his great love for her and his determination that this oppression be lessened, weighed more heavily upon her both in spirit and body as she grew older.

V   A Summing Up

Maupassant, then, is a precursor of the modern literature which regards war's permanence as resultant to the people's unwillingness to abandon the old myths that treat of pride and heroics. But to see him in this role one must read all he has had to say on the subject—not just a few celebrated stories whose bright intensity keeps us from seeing other important attitudes lurking behind. He regarded war's immortality to be directly related to man's worship. He knew that the god of war could, and should, be brought down to the mortal plain. But he despaired of its ever happening. For one thing the wealthy, the class of leaders, used the myths of honor and glory to keep themselves supplied with gun-fodder. And for another, that very prospective gun-fodder was, as a body, too simple to realize how it was being used until it was all over. The few *individuals* among the masses would not be enough to slay the many-headed dragon, so that being one of those rare individuals gave him neither a sense of hope nor pride, only dismay.

As much as the war meant to him as a writer, Maupassant's unequivocal denunciations of it in *Sur l'Eau* show how very great a role the matter of his brief and unillustrious service in the army at the time of the Franco-Prussian War had upon formulating his ideas afterward. The effect is quite out of proportion to his exposure to war. But Maupassant reveals here both the quality of his spirit and the powers of his imagination to make much of very little: he needed to see but little to grasp the moral corruption that is the foment of war; only the briefest skirmish could serve him as the inspiration for an expertly detailed analysis of the behavior of troops or civilians in time of war. The moral questions which war raises are especially well articulated: "Just the thought of the word, war, and I am thrown into a state of bewilderment as if one were talking about witchcraft, of inquiring about a very remote thing, about something that was over and done, of an abomination, a monstrosity against nature" (XVIII, 52). There is an indignant tone in these denunciations that is traditional in French satire: "War! . . . To fight! . . . To cut men's throats! . . . To massacre them! . ." (XV, 53–54).

The hopelessness and pessimism that pervaded Maupassant's thinking both as a result of Flaubert's instruction and his own penchants are well expressed in his astonishment that the people are such cattle. Why don't they rise up against governments? "Oh, But we shall always live beneath the weight of old and odious customs, of criminal prejudices, of the ferocious ideas of our barbaric forefathers, for we are beasts, we shall remain beasts, dominated by instinct and oblivious to any change" (XVIII, 54).

Maupassant does not spare the politicians and the generals. In that respect he is very modern and, as well, a link with all of the past satires of the pomposity and heartlessness of war lords and generals. "Men of war are the scourges of the world" (XVIII, 56).

But in the final analysis, what concerned him deepest was the debilitating effect of war on the positive efforts, few though they were, to form governments where social justice was a reality. Wars caused men to draw themselves together because of social, political, religious, or racial interests. It destroyed the last vestiges of civility:

When the law no longer exists, is dead, when every notion of what is just disappears, we see innocents mowed down in roadways and under suspicion just because they are afraid. No one has the absolute right to govern others. Whoever does govern has as strong a duty to avoid war as a ship's captain has to avoid shipwreck.

Maupassant did not have faith in a truculent government's ability to avoid shipwreck for its people. He had seen too much of his own government.

A forlorn hope with Maupassant was that some day man would have sufficient inner vision to turn the weapons his government had given him for offensive maneuvers against other simple people upon the warlords who had provided them.

CHAPTER 6

Madness—Inspirer, Daily Companion, and Death-Dealer

I The Haunting Specter

MORE than its fatal triumph, the long term of the stay of madness in the mind of Maupassant should be considered by the Maupassant critic. The extensive history of its development is not only evident in his work, but its slow progress inspired some of the finest work. Madness must be seen in its role as a shaper of certain of his writings. He knew quite early in his career that he was in the fatal grip of madness, and the realization caused him to turn his attention to the pathological behavior in himself as a vital source for his fiction. Even the casual reader of Maupassant has likely encountered several stories in which madness plays the vital role. But there are many in which the insanity is a subtle reflection of his personal struggles with the malady.

Maupassant was able to conceive of that little bit of madness in us all because he was a little more than "normally" mad, and his characters all have that human degree of madness which gives them reality and causes us to identify with them. His occasional treatments of madness as the central issue in a story, then, tell but a small part of the drama of how it plagued his literary career from beginning to end. Plagued it and aided it! For his fears and his aberrations are the protoplasm of his characters, all of whom are exaggerated in that enchanting way that makes it possible for a reader to enjoy literature and at the same time not regard it as pure fantasy. To assume that madness was important solely at the end of his career is to fail to grasp how his fears and superstitions concerning his malady are fed into the characters he creates, not merely for the sake of literary creativity, but also that he might observe their appearance and growth and thereby understand them in himself. His unusual

103

perceptiveness concerning madness increased because of the extraordinarily long period thoughts of his own malady held him
at bay.

Premonitions of his troubles appear in the psychological turmoil of many of his early characters. When lined up they present
almost a journal of the developments of the illness that was working sinisterly upon the mind of their creator. Maupassant must
have been conscious of the fact that he was narrating his own
difficulties, and of the future ramifications of such experiences;
for he tried at every turn to reject the notion that the signs per-
tained to him personally. Even with Hervé's madness, he was
not about to see how closely the symptoms of his brother's disease
paralleled his own, symptoms he had already treated so startlingly
in his works. But the more he tried to appear perfectly sound
to himself and to others, the more clearly did his masquerade
reveal that he was not. And there were those who were quick to
make cruel note of it.

It was not until 1886 that Maupassant wrote *Le Horla*. Its
outstanding strangeness has inspired a number of celebrated
theories as to how it is the evocation of his personal mental
instability. But too few of the theorists responsible care to explore the steps of increasing psychological stress which can be
seen outlined in the stories prior to its appearance. *Le Horla*, the
visitor, was not the creature of sudden fears; the idea for "him"
had been developing in his mind all along. Its slow gestation can
be seen in the earlier presentations of disturbed characters. Just
as we have observed so often, the idea worked itself through a
series of lesser stages of perfection before reaching its most
dramatic realization. Repetition is a phenomenon in Maupassant
with which we are prepared to live because we can see through
the various redactions the progress toward a perfect articulation;
Maupassant is far from the kind of writer who says the same
thing over for lack of anything else to say. The notoriety of *Le
Horla* tends to dazzle us so that we do not see all the works behind it and of which it represents the perfect culmination. In
the beginning he had treated madness as someone else's problem;
Le Horla treats madness as his own problem.

To trace the progress of a theme in Maupassant's work is to
trace its course in his own life. Here, then, we shall study the

most tortured, fear-filled moments of his life that find their reflection in his work. There is no way to appreciate the events of a writer's life without finding the key to the personality that lived it. What Maupassant had to say on the subject of the Realist's task in the introduction to *Boule de Suif* is certainly put into practice as he deals with this subject which became for him a terrifying reality. "We have this singular objective; the Being and the Life, that one must know how to understand and interpret as an artist. If one does not give at the same time an exact and artistically superior expression of it, it is because one hasn't enough talent" (IV, 84–85).

Loneliness was a major factor in the development of Maupassant's affliction. Living too much to himself, he formed certain ideas whose very inalterability was their poison. The exactness with which Maupassant described Madame de Guilleroy's loneliness in *Fort Comme la Mort* results from his experience with the problem. "Fixed ideas have the tenacity of gnawing, incurable maladies. Once entered into the mind, they devour it, leave it no longer free to think of anything, to be interested in anything, or to have an inclination in the slightest toward anything" (XIV, 277). Maynial has explained the steady progress of madness in Maupassant's work in the following manner: "The man who delivers to the public his clear vision of the world has not yet suffered from life, but he has certainly suffered inwardly from a mysterious disquietude that he does not wish to admit to himself and that he pours out in spite of himself throughout his lucid and conscientiously wrought prose."[1] Solitude became a morbid passion with Maupassant in his latter days. Like Dostoevskian characters his creations sought what they most feared and were rewarded with terrifying visions and hallucinations. Their behavior has its convincing psychological profundity from the fact that it is a mirroring of his own.

Throughout his life we can see him agreeing with more passionate intensity with the hero of *La Question du Latin*: "Ah! my dear fellow, a key, a key to a door that one can close and lock, that's happiness, that's the only happiness" (XVI, 255). But when he had found the key and locked himself in he became a prey to visitors such as the mysterious second self who presents himself to the heroes of *Le Horla* and *Lui?*

And then, too, he has another character, Christiane, of *Mont-Oriol* make the case for the inevitability of loneliness and it sounds strangely like Sartre:

She understood that even in that man's arms, when she had felt herself mingled with him, entered into him, when she had felt that their flesh and souls formed no longer but a single flesh and single soul, they had but slightly approached one another enough to cause their impenetrable envelopes in which mysterious nature has isolated and closed humans to touch. She saw clearly that no one has ever been or will be able to break that invisible barrier which puts beings as far from one another in life as are the stars in heaven. (XVIII, 410)

And yet loneliness lay so heavily upon the last half decade of his life that Maupassant could repudiate this testimony of his heroine which came very close to winding up his case against marriage, suggesting that it was better to be blatantly hypocritical and accept conventions one detested than to be alone. The hero of *Lui?*, as we shall later remark, was almost surely invented after Maupassant had battled with himself over the inconsistencies in his attitudes toward celibacy and marriage.

Solitude leads to suicide Maupassant shows us in *Suicides*. It was loneliness that caused the heroine of *Miss Harriet* to cast herself into the well. Fortunately for us, Maupassant was not entirely alone; he had François Tassart who kept an eye on him and was there to thwart his suicide attempts. Old Monsieur Parent, despite bitterness at having been cuckolded, still could not abide the lonely nights. More and more Maupassant seems to have been aware of the approaching end. His increasing personal terror of the night signals the madness that was perhaps as much the result of loneliness as it was of the physical disease which racked him. The night falls upon his characters' hearts "like a mist of chagrin, an inundation of despair." And, like Baudelaire, as much as he despised the lazy, ambitionless wallow of humanity, he had to go in search of his fellow beings.

II *A Desperate Search for the Cure*

The narrator of *Solitude* expresses the pessimism that is characteristic of Maupassant's last years, stating that the sole recompense for the lonely man is "the egotistical satisfaction of understanding, of seeing, of divining, and of suffering interminably from recognition of our eternal isolation" (XXI, 263). The shade of Flaubert is here, influencing his disciple to suggest that we are all in a desert where no one understands anyone else and where the distances between us remain greater than those between the stars. The steady focus of this pessimistic view upon his deliberations left it impossible for him to find a solution; for never did he believe strongly enough that there would be anyone else who could come remotely close to being the kind of soul mate for him that he had found in Flaubert. The only person whose presence gave him the sense of not being alone had been Flaubert. How could he really have solved the problem, then, by choosing a wife? He would have still been alone and afraid of himself. Nor are we ever assured that his heroes who seize marriage as a solution to the problem of loneliness did indeed find it so. The suggestion is that they did not.

There are the lights, the people. Where they are one can at least delude himself into thinking he is not alone as does the hero of *Garçon, un Bock* who will not abandon the bistro until its last sparks of light and conversation have been extinguished. Maupassant, who did not surrender to the temptation to catch someone and tell his tale as did the hero of *La Ficelle*, or the Ancient Mariner, nevertheless was able to portray with great psychological perception the spirit that moves certain among the race to do so. That he did not surrender personally to the temptation does not rule out the probability that these unhappy wretches of his who do relate the ills of their loneliness are really manifestations of himself. Their neuroses are in many cases those he controlled or suppressed. When the hero of *Garçon, un Bock* tells how his mother was murdered by his brute of a father who was enraged at not being allowed to squander the last penny of the family's money, one is tempted to see how this could be an exaggerated rendition of the state of affairs existing between his own mother and father. Loneliness has but lacerated the wounds of the narrator so that he, like Maupassant himself, can no longer abide the thought of having to suffer from them in silence and solitude.

The strange fears and premonitions that built themselves in the author's mind over the years and contributed to the severity of his malady are evident in his earliest writings, as well as in the later ones. And hence his literary output from one end to the other reveals the progress of the dark tide that swept over him at the last. Most of the time the theme of madness is not at flood tide, but is only a sinister undertow. Maupassant's biography would be incomplete were it not to include all of the great influences of his life: along with his mother, ships, and sailing, and the loss of direction and sense of purpose that led up to the defeat in the Franco-Prussian War and their influence on the totality of his life and work was the presence of an ever-evolving concern about madness. Its long history can only be surmised from a study of his work; and it matters little whether Laure de Maupassant suppressed information pertaining to this latter subject or whether Maupassant failed to discuss it more thoroughly in his correspondence than a few remaining letters show, there is simply little direct discussion of the problem except through the words of his characters. Maupassant's contention that the writer alone is capable of judging the validity of his subject matter which depends upon what he knows how to write leads to the interesting speculation that Maupassant's knowledge of madness was first-hand and that, if he did not avow it openly, he confessed it unintentionally.

Even the earliest period, when the future short-story writer and novelist considered his destiny to lie in poetry, there appear in his poems ominous portents of what is to insinuate itself in his life. The 1880 volume of lyric and narrative poems contains one entitled, "Terreur." Several lines read like the later stories on madness: "That evening I had been reading for a very long time some author. / It was exactly midnight, and suddenly I was afraid. / Of what?" The rest tells of how his fear that someone was watching him from behind and laughing softly caused him to faint from terror. True, all of us have had some such eerie feelings when immersed in reading a terrifying story. But with Maupassant this scene repeats itself throughout his work so as to reveal an obsession with it. And later the someone peering over his shoulder is the autoscopic double whose arrival in his life and work signaled the gravity of his illness.

By 1882 there were more indications of the mounting malady. *Rêves*, published in July of that year, tells of a group of men indulging in the then fashionable decadent pastime of discovering an unthought-of vice. There is the suggestion that the use of drugs under Baudelaire's influence provides a gateway to such discovery, to which a physician present responds that he who would supply ether for such experiments would contribute to a man's self-destruction. Fear of becoming addicted to the ether, which he took to relieve the terrible migraines he experienced, likely prompted Maupassant to create the physician and his advice. As far as is known, the hallucinations the author experienced were the result of a number of nervous disorders and overindulgences in things other than his medication.

III   *The Fearful Observer—The "Sane" Watching the "Mad"*

In August, 1882, he focused upon the subject of criminal madness. The interrogation point in the title, *Fou?* is most significant in revealing Maupassant's reluctance to judge a man mad. The story consists of a fascinating study of a man who, like Keats' pale knight, has been in the grip of "la belle dame sans merci." "I loved that woman with a frenzied impulse. . . . But is that really so? Did I love her? No, no, no. She possessed me body and soul, invaded me, tied herself to me. I was and am her thing, her toy . . . she is the *woman of perdition,* the sensual and false animal for whom the soul does not exist" (italics mine) (X, 115–16).

Out of his mind with the certainty of losing her, he lived in a perpetual state of frenzied jealousy. Her daily horseback rides (remembrances of *Madame Bovary*) he suspects are for the purposes of meeting a lover; and then even worse suspicions besiege him, and he takes vengeance upon the horse by breaking its legs and allowing it to suffer. Afterward he turns upon the enraged woman and kills her. Another example of how Maupassant sees the madman as always having his story on his lips and in search of a listener, he opens and closes this narrative with the incessant question, "Am I a madman?"

It appears that Maupassant wishes to suggest that the provocation justified the crime. If the man is truly mad it is only the woman's fault, and it was right that she be punished. Maupassant makes this rare mention of the "femme fatale" in his large work. He, himself, never fell under her influence, it seems certain, for he made a fetish of dominating any woman he could and of avoiding entanglements with any whose effect upon him hinted at a capacity for dominance. It was his interest in madness and all of its possible origins that attracted him to include her this once in his work.

All varieties of madness attract him, and his fine comprehension of the nuances of each type can but be related to his growing realization of his own condition and his fears regarding what will be its final issue. It is notable that in 1882 he began calling a madman by his name *"fou."* From that year on his interest in this tortured creature grows with frightening significance.

In October *La Peur* appeared. The story provides a significant correlative to Maupassant's life of that year. In the first place its various anecdotes are inspired by his own reaction to the dark continent whose mystery and savagery had for him an attraction similar to that of so many physically powerful and lusty writers such as he and Hemingway, for example, were. Maupassant was inordinately proud of his physical prowess and courage, and yet like many such men he began to be dominated by a strange fear of a power over his life against which all of his strength, courage, and intelligence would be of no avail. He regarded most ordinary men as being immune to such fears. Their minds were used up completely by the normal fears of coming to some accidental bodily harm, or of failure.

Maupassant's intelligence and imagination caused him to pass far beyond such primal fears: he grew to fear the very *uniqueness* of the eye trouble that caused him such pain; and it appeared to him that some special force had taken up the challenge of making his life a torment. He was fiercely romantic in feeling that, in order to instill fear into the life of such a man as he, a god would gladly abandon the flock of lesser men and concentrate a part of his eternity solely upon the accomplishment. When he later felt that the society of intellectuals, the writers, and the editors were continually putting their energies and brains to the task of belittling him and destroying him he was unafraid. But with this god whom he considered to be dedicated to the specific task of doing him in it was different; his pursuer, being above men, would be able to come into his life under the most clever disguises, and at the moment most auspicious for his plans. And so we begin to have Maupassant wrestling with the fear of not being able to cope with the demon whose coming his mind has prophesied. Later, indeed, his fear is realized in *Le Horla* and others of his stories.

La Peur gives us a glimpse of the immobilizing power of fear, an actual accounting of how without the slightest basis in reason it can grow into a fatal sickness. The story also provides us with an insight into what the interior life of the author was gradually becoming. His real enemy was fear, just as the story shows us. To see how foolishly the mind can twist a perfectly logical, friendly shape into a terrifying one does nothing to keep the mind from repeating the mistake; one does not learn by his mistakes where fear is concerned. Fear is a specter sleeping in the mind which needs but the slightest nudge to be awakened. Maupassant is clearly speaking of his own mental state in the story when he has one of the conversants point out how much easier it is for man to confront a pressing and visible danger, no matter how evident are the odds against victory, than to oppose the force that has no substance, being the product of an exaggerated imagination. What happens to a man in a state of fear is "a decomposition of the soul" (VIII, 75). The logical explanation of the drums of death the travelers among the Sahara dunes hear comes too late: the decomposition has already occurred, the damage done. The same is true when the "dead man" glowering in the window turns out to be a dog left in the bitter cold. Fear lingered in those who were the witnesses to these things. At this point Maupassant could still regard these, his creations, as "others," but soon he would be incapable of distinguishing his emotions from theirs.

IV   *On First Contemplating the Insane*

By March, 1883, Maupassant's interest in insanity was no longer something he wished to disguise in his stories. It emerged just as distinctly as did his eminence in the field of letters. *Mademoiselle Cocotte* with its modern reliance upon the atmosphere of an insane asylum and the clinical record of one of the patients for its setting and narrative, introduces the reader to a man who talks incessantly with an imaginary dog. Madness, Maupassant tells us, is triggered in each of us differently: *one goes mad for his own reasons.* This man's madness resulted from his betrayal of the slavish devotion of a mongrel bitch dog in order to satisfy his superior. The dog's extraordinary procreation

due to the fact that she "shared her favors with the indifference
of a girl" angered the peasant's master who demanded the animal
be destroyed. The order to kill this good and innocent creature,
to betray its love for expediency's sake, was too much for the
peasant; he went mad. The parallel with the way humans interact
is quite neatly suggested, though the primary point of the story
is but to give a simple recounting of the steps to one man's
madness.

A month after this story appeared, Maupassant turned again
to a study of fear in *Apparition*. He had a fine, instinctive knowledge of psychology, and on top of that a mounting series of
personal fears and frightful hallucinations to move him to study
the place of fear's role in the destruction of the healthy mind. In
this story the narrator cannot without terror recall an experience
of over a half century past. He had promised a friend to retrieve
some papers from the room of the latter's dead wife. In the room
he heard terrible sighs and saw the ghost of the dead woman,
who commanded him to comb her long flowing hair so as to
relieve her suffering. (Biographical note: Maupassant is said to
have experienced relief from his migraines whenever his hair was
brushed.) After the apparition has vanished, long strands of
hair remained clinging to his clothes. The narrator's fears concerning the occurrence brought a shade of madness into his life.

April, 1883, was an important date for Maupassant. *Une Vie*
appeared and with it Maupassant's conviction that it proved he
was a novelist. But it too contains passages that show how un-
relentingly the mind of the author was pursuing the question of
madness. The heroine, Jeanne, experiences mental disorders
which are very nearly fatal and which resemble in many respects
a great many that came to light in Maupassant's own later life. It
is quite reasonable to suppose that the state of her mental health
measures in many respects the state of Maupassant's own at the
time of the writing.

Frequently it has been stated that one of Maupassant's phobias
concerned the certainty of aging and that the magnitude of his
fears concerning the phenomenon was disproportionate to that
experienced even by most highly sensitive people. He perhaps
knew that he was to experience old age without ever really becoming old in years; for he tortured himself unmercifully with
thoughts of a senile slackening of productivity and discipline. He

feared the prospect of living with himself as an old man. Ironically, it was only as he began to be preoccupied with this theme
of aging that he wished to obey rigidly the admonitions of his
late master, Flaubert, not to waste himself upon any activity
that did not contribute to his work. Memories of how he had
refused to take Flaubert seriously now came home to haunt him
and to further jeopardize the precarious mental balance of the
last decade of his life. "There is nothing more terrible," he
observes in *Une Vie,* "when one is old, than to stick one's nose
back into his youth" (II, 228).

Like Maupassant, the heroine of *Une Vie* vacillated between
a desire to return to visit with the ghosts of her mother and father
and a terror of finding what she had not known was there before.
She pursued her past with an ambivalence resembling that of
the heroes in *Lui?* and *Le Horla* as they sought their second
selves. What she found very often was as recognizable as a
piece of Maupassant's biography as it was of her own. She sensed
her dead mother's presence; she too experienced the hallucinations Maupassant was so concerned with: "Jeanne thought she
felt a breath flutter over her, like the contact with a spirit. *She
was afraid,* atrociously so, so violently struck that she dared not
move, nor breathe, nor turn around to peer behind her" (II, 239).
The rooms of her house resembled Baudelaire's "Flacon"; from
them surged forth the perfumes of happier days: "She believed
she saw, she did see, as she had so often, her father and her
mother warming their feet by the fire" (II, 314).

April, 1883, was kind to Maupassant, that is, insofar as getting
his work in print was concerned. But his work reveals his cruel,
relentless progress during this season toward madness. Suicide
was on his mind. *Une Vie* had been peopled with characters with
a suicide bent, and the story *Suicides* presented a penetrating
analysis of the consistently prevalent cult. What Maupassant did
was to present an apology for the act of taking one's own life.
His feeling that there are strong and valid reasons for self-
destruction and his sympathy for suicide's victims sound like
the thoughts of a man whose understanding has been gained
through studying it as a possible ultimate for himself. And, of
course, with hindsight, we can be relatively sure that such a
thought was in his mind. His own later attempt was likely
predicated upon the logic he had developed in this analysis.

Fortunately, despite his furious efforts to prove himself a man of action by creating a sort of "he-man" image, Maupassant was very much a Hamlet: thought counted far more to him than action as long as he was able to exercise his thought faculties with direction and effectively.

The story, *Suicides,* bares the contents of the letter written by one of those labeled by society as a "senseless self-murderer." It is a most interesting letter, in which again the role of loneliness in inducing madness is stressed. (How much more than he ever told must Maupassant have suffered while pretending to prefer to be left alone!) The disintegrating into madness is outlined in the letter as "the fatal disorganization of a solitary existence" (XXVI, 230). Maupassant waged a continuing battle against this "fatal disorganization" that his own solitary existence threatened to impose upon his own life. From the beginning his robust nature had revolted against asceticism and solitude. Perhaps a part of his cracking under the strain of loneliness was due to the need in early life to be a part of the active world. Maupassant's terror of being alone *with himself* is the most characteristic fear of the last decade of his life; his aversion to solitude in his younger years was what Flaubert had correctly analyzed as a dangerous proclivity of many talented people to spend their lives among others talking and gathering ideas and information more as a manner of avoiding the lonely task of shaping them into a form whose very art would assure their communication to others than for the sake of enhancing their understanding or broadening their vision. Early, loneliness had meant being *by himself;* later it came to mean being *with himself.* He was the kind of individual for whom the latter state, though necessary for his particular work, often has fatal consequences.

The letter writer's words provide a foreboding of what must have been Maupassant's thoughts when he contemplated suicide. The hero has decided to kill himself because of an awareness of the irremediable brutality of existence in which he has failed to find a single strain of poetry his youthful naïveté has assigned to it: "We are the eternal playthings of ever renewing, stupid, and charming illusions" (XXVI, 231). The foregoing outcry sums up neatly what Emma Bovary was incapable of understanding and hence articulating. *Flaubert's influence is never far distant.* The statement is also in complete accord with Maupassant's disillusionment with life that is so prominent a factor both in his work and in his mental difficulties.

For his fictional creation, even travel gave no release from the dull rerun of life. Travel was dear to Maupassant, but it also let him down as he became more and more a prisoner of the aberrations symptomatic of madness. The strong probability that the author experienced the turmoils with which he invests his characters is accepted by Maynial, who observed: "There is scarcely a book of Maupassant, between 1884 and 1890, in which one does not find that morbid passion for solitude."[2] Like his hero, Maupassant saw himself destined to wander hopelessly among the discouraging truths his intelligence could not help from presenting him, truths which concealed brutally all the dreams and ideals of his happy childhood. If life is but such a senseless wandering about in one's own disappointing revelations, then is it not the "rational" thing to do to take one's life? Maupassant often causes us to ponder the question of who is mad; is it really the man whose actions seem abnormal, or isn't it the one who is too dull to perceive the insanity of idle contentment? He believed that all reaction was condemned as madness by those who wished to impose the idea that "sane," "logical" behavior consisted in silent acceptance. But such reasonings are very often fabricated by the man who wishes to defend himself against accusations of madness, and the fact that Maupassant resorts to them indicates that he was not, after all, much less concerned with the world's opinion than the majority of mankind.

The year 1883 must have been the one in which Maupassant faced squarely the inevitability of the presence of an extraordinary ingredient in his life that would bring him to an end not common among men. The vision only caused him to redouble his efforts to avoid classing himself with men who suffered from mental disorders. Evidence of the presaging is the monthly parade of stories dealing with madness. In June came *Lui?* The hero's kinship to his creator is borne out clearly by the former's wishing to defend himself for marrying after having established a reputation for being an ardent foe of marriage. Maupassant, as has been noted, cried out vigorously against marriage but relented in his attacks in later years because of his exorbitant fear of being alone. The only times in his life he ever considered marriage seriously were moments when his inner debate led him to the conclusion that something terrible would transpire, a thing far more terrible than putting up with a wife.

"Yes, I'm marrying," admits the hero. But he assures his auditor that it is not the result of a change in philosophy: "I consider legal mating to be an absurdity" (XXVI, 93). Maupassant makes identical statements in his travel journals as well as in his fiction. The certainty of the coming of the banal state of marriage is perhaps a comforting prospect for a man with psychotic inclinations for whom uncertainty is feared excessively. It would seem an exaggeration to suggest that Maupassant would have been willing to be bored to death as opposed to facing all of the phantoms a troubled imagination can give life to. Nevertheless, Maupassant's fears were such at certain times during the last ten years of his life that at those times he would have willingly spent his nights with the dullest of mates. Clearly, the hero is but Maupassant watching himself and listening to himself talk almost as if it were the autoscopic hallucination which his hero is about to relate. "I got married so as not to be alone. I want to feel a being near me, against me, a being who can speak, say something, it matters not what" (XXVI, 95).

The desperate frenzy of the hero's search for no matter what kind of female companion is justified: he had been the victim of an autoscopic hallucination. On returning to his empty house after having spent an evening searching for a friend to visit, he found his favorite chair before the fire occupied—on approaching to touch the stranger seated there he felt but empty air; it had been himself whom he had seen. His frantic efforts never to be alone were futile: he always found too much time to dream and redream the experience. He tells of a new and frightening trouble with his *eyes* which further justifies a biographer's studying the story as an authentic autobiographical fragment: "I was afraid I'd see it again, him. Not fear of him, not fear of his presence, in which I didn't believe, *but I was afraid of a new trouble with my eyes, afraid of the hallucination, afraid of the fear that would seize me*" (italics mine) (XXVI, 104). To marry and reject completely the rationale he had developed against marriage is, to him, a surrender to madness. But the knowledge of what he has encountered, his memory of the experience, and the possibility of its repeating itself unbalanced him. "It haunts me. I know it's crazy, but that's the way it is" (XXVI, 105). It is always a threat that the lonely man will encounter this double, especially if he has neurotic symptoms such as extreme sensibility and nervousness, megalomania, a pathological pride in real or imagined powers, or if he has been indulgent in sex. Little doubt can there be that Maupassant had reason to put these strange words in the mouth of his hero: *"For he is there because I am alone, uniquely because I am alone"* (italics mine) (XXVI, 196).

V *A Positive and a Negative Force*

Maynial summarizes the ambivalent attitudes in Maupassant that are at once the imaginative forces responsible for many of his works and the forces which accelerated the deterioration of his mind. An ambivalence regarding solitude made its way into Maupassant's thinking when the lessons Flaubert had sought to teach him began to make sense: the man who wrote required much solitude for the accomplishment of his task. He began to love and hate being alone. Fear played such a predominant role in his life that he was inevitably turned toward the decadent "love for and the cult of fear."[3] Maynial credits fear especially with being the villain: "Fear entered into him, it possessed him, it dominated him, and what is better, it attracted him, charmed him and held him in a sort of state of perverse enchantment."[4]

Suicide appears again in *Le Petit* of August, 1883. The cuckold, for whom, as we have seen, Maupassant had the greatest scorn, is here treated sympathetically. "He was a good man, true fellow, simple, quite simple, sincere, without defiance and without malice" (XXVII, 199). Almost as unusual is the author's turning upon the cuckolder herself for whom he more typically, as we have seen, would offer a defense. The hero, a widower at the instant of becoming a father, fastened himself to the boy with a fanatical, sick love, spoiled the child's chances of developing normally, disposing it to wild temper tantrums at the hint of correction. His insane worship and the maid's determination to discipline the child came into conflict, and seeing herself dismissed she informed him that the man with whom he had always shared his last crust was the child's father. And, as in *Pierre et Jean,* a portrait confirms what the naïve man would not have believed otherwise. The shock posed too great a strain on his mind. He forgot his mad passion to provide for the child in the far more urgent madness of extinguishing his personal agony.

Maupassant's bitter, ever-growing conviction that one's goodness is but the very instrument his enemy will use to destroy him,
can be seen in the manner in which he leads his hero to madness
and suicide. More and more Maupassant's writing of the period
studies men who believe they have learned that misrepresenta-
tion and treachery are the means whereby one survives, and being incapable of these or of subsisting in a world where they rule,
they retreat into a life of madness or find an immediate exit in
suicide. The persistence of this sort of problem in his stories
shows very well the troubled state of his own thoughts during
the time.

Suicide, like the other facets of demented behavior, challenged
Maupassant the storyteller: he wished to probe its motivations
in a manner that would reveal its closeness to all men. In this
way it served as a regenerative force. He was always angered by
the petty fears that stem from cowardice. The fears of most of
his characters are dignified, represent "manly fears," and there is
no hint in them of the base fears that pale the conscience of
cowards.

The first month of 1884, however, saw the publication of a
study of a suicide which stemmed directly from the hero's lack
of courage to face the consequences of having posed as a brave
man. *Un Lâche* is a typical Maupassantian attack on the myth of
male courage and resolve. He made those who insisted on displaying their manhood where there was no danger, face danger;
he put the brave talkers to test. He treated these themes because
it angered him to live in a world where all was a sham. Vicomte
Gontran, who poses as a brave, resolute man, is a coward, who
cannot face up to the duel he has bargained for. (The same episode appears in *Bel-Ami.*) Maupassant's *"lâche"* is significant
because of his interesting self-analysis. Failure to measure up to
his expectation of himself leads the hero to study himself. Like
so many heroes of the great nineteenth-century novels, the moment of truth is but a ploy in order to arrange for the central
theme which is self-psychoanalysis. Maupassant favored these debates between the hero and himself strongly during the latter
part of his career. We can reasonably assume that Maupassant's
mania for proving himself led him to the same sort of interior
debates and analyses. He, too, was unprepared for failure in
feats of strength or stamina, or literature. But they came. And

one must suppose that he dealt with them in much the same way his characters do.

To discover that one has erred all along in assessing his noble attributes can have a shock capable of producing madness. The hero of *Un Lâche* had never dared admit to himself that he was a coward. The story deals with the process of self-discovery and the effect of the turmoil of discovery. "He felt an insane need to roll on the floor, to weep, to bite" (XXVII, 117). The one thing a coward will not admit is his cowardice. Gontran follows the pattern. There is nothing for him but suicide.

Maupassant regards the extreme fear of being found out for what one is as a sickness, a madness. Perhaps this is why he was such an exhibitionist: he feared that refraining from exhibiting manhood, sexual prowess, and the like was merely a blank wall behind which all was equally blank. He wanted to be found out for what he was. Maupassant was, contrary to this hero, never disappointed in what he found himself to be. But he made a fetish of testing himself, a madness that contributed to the greater madness that doomed him.

Insanity provided him with inspiration again in May, 1884. Yet another visit to an asylum turns up a hero. How familiar Maupassant was becoming with asylums! In his fiction he visited their inmates, and in real life he visited his brother, Hervé, in such a place, and in his dreams he feared that he should also meet himself there someday. His morbid interest drove him forward to further study of insanity. It seems that he was searching for something that he knew he must uncover before his powers to analyze it had abandoned him. Each new case is interesting and imaginative, but none of them slaked his thirst for knowledge on the subject. In *La Chevelure* the patient is intermittently raging and calm. The doctor describes his malady as follows: "He is besieged by an erotic, macabre madness" (XXIX, 120). The patient's diary unfolds a bizarre story of necrophilism. Like his creator, he had had a morbid fear of falling in love, and so he stayed away from women. The passing of time haunted him, frightened him so that he could not find a sane manner to put it to use. There was not the kind of genius that could arrest it with a work of art. Ennui conquered resolve: "But it passes, it passes, it takes a little bit of me from second to second for tomorrow's nothingness. And I shall never live again" (XXIX, 122–23). Unable to employ creativity as insurance against time's rapid flow, he turned to what others had done, collecting anything for the sake of having it, touching it, feeling he was in the presence of time arrested. An antique desk with a secret drawer containing tresses of blond hair provided him with an occasion to imagine again what were the fingers that had caressed them lovingly and what beauty had possessed them and how they had ended up in his possession tugging with them a vague past. His last obsession as a sane man was the desire to have them in his hands at all times. Madness convinced him that the woman had come to him to be his wife. He became quite wild and had to be put away. The asylum attendants confiscated the locks and drove the wretch further into the lonely darkness of his insanity. Maupassant had the doctor close with an ironic pronouncement that was later often to be heard maliciously spoken about him: "The mind of man is capable of anything" (XXIX, 131).

VI *Who Is Mad and Who Is Sane?*

La Peur (July, 1884) asks the question that haunted Maupassant the artist during the last decade of his life when he felt that his critics misunderstood him and were maliciously working against his reputation. More and more misanthropic, he felt that adverse criticisms stemmed from the wrongness of others, that there could be little quibbling with the rightness of his own position. In his stories he answers those who are casting doubt upon his sanity: "But does one know the wise from the madmen, in this life where reason ought often to be labeled foolishness and madness genius?" (XXIX, 267). (For the student of contemporary literature, what better way to establish his kinship and influence?) The old man who narrates the story makes a pronouncement that was often on Maupassant's lips and on the lips of many another writer of tales of the unknown and the world of supernatural beings: "Yes, my dear sir, they depopulated the imagination by suppressing the invisible" (XXIX, 268).

Maupassant's interest in psychology increased markedly during the last part of his career as a writer. Though, as has been suggested, he comes through particularly well as a sound observer of the mind throughout his work, at this time he became interested in the technical data of the psychologist and wished to write psychological novels to rival those of Paul Bourget, whom he admired. The narrator of *La Peur* is fascinated by the kind of psychological pattern capable of bringing into view the terrible things that lie at the extremities of the imagination. These people with their visions that brand them as mad in the eyes of their hearers, the narrator (author) views as less mad than those who call them mad. To deny the presence of the ghosts they see, to refuse to admit the existence of the fears they evince is to deny the existence of such things, and to deny their existence is to deprive man of the wealth of literature for which they are responsible: "Along with the supernatural, true fear disappeared from the earth, *for one is truly afraid only of what he doesn't understand*" (italics mine).

If one can believe he has come to terms with the mysteries of his life, whether or not he really has, he can live what is termed a normal life. Sensitive people have a hard time deluding themselves. Maupassant possessed the kind of sensitivity which denied him the satisfaction of coming to terms, and although it provided him with the impetus for much of his work, it hastened his mental deterioration. He had great admiration for what he regarded as Turgenev's unique capacity for forcing upon his reader's mind the reality of a shadowy unknown and leaving him with the eerie feeling that there is SOMETHING behind the door, the wall. His narrator praises the Russian: "He doesn't boldly enter into the supernatural as Poe or Hoffmann do, he tells simple stories where there mingles something a bit vague and troubling" (XXIX, 270). Understanding prevents the unknown from making madmen of us all. The narrator tells of becoming frenzied to the point of jeopardizing his sanity by the sight of a wheelbarrow appearing to roll by itself. In such a case a certain kind of mind allows imagination to cancel curiosity, so that one makes in his mind a reality of what is indeed not a reality. And he goes on to explain that fear of the plague is a product of the imagination. For it is not that one thinks of it as what it really is, but one gives to it a brain, the ruthlessness of a bloody barbarian of the Orient from which it comes, a capacity for bringing itself back from the dead of ages past where it had been born and had lived. The narrator's analysis of fear is Maupassant's.

There is no wonder Maupassant attaches so much importance in his stories to a study of fear; for in rendering the thesis that fear is the product of the imagination which will not permit us time to be sufficiently curious, he only makes it more evident how doomed he was to failure in coping with his own fears, against which no amount of curiosity was of any avail. They were not in any way related to the physical world where curiosity can halt a runaway imagination before it destroys the mind; his fears were related to the other world where the imagination provides the only life and possesses the only entrance key. Fear he realized was every man's cohabitant; Maupassant was too sensitive, possessed too fine a mind not to probe any part of his existence to the fullest extent possible. Where others could find the external world sufficiently distracting to allow them to ignore the beast within, he could not. It took courage. And in the end the endeavor to retrace his steps to the material world was futile. Fear of his condition, his battling against its overwhelming superiority with the slow realization that it was destined to win, gave Maupassant the determination to see it through and the insight that lends his studies of madness their convincing quality and their pathos. It seems that the light he creates in the struggles of his characters illuminates for him his own. His creations depend upon him for light, and he, in turn, depends upon their flashes for discoveries of the "himself" he still does not understand or know.

The origin of madness is a distinct concern expressed in Maupassant's work of the year 1884. It appears again he was determined to show that madness under certain conditions is the only "sane" approach to life. He was concerned with his own mental health and had had numerous opportunities to examine his personal phobias and psychoses—the same ones in many cases which he gives to his characters who can afford to act more dramatically than he who created them but who still regarded himself as capable of triumphing over the accumulation of woes that had brought them down. Maupassant, with a spate of critics who harbored more and more malice toward a man who had seldom tried to disguise his growing contempt and desire to withdraw from them, was quite aware that it would be damaging to show outward signs of his distress. But he often gives us heroes whose strange behavior the narrator begins by regarding much as the average person would, with a certain revulsion mingled with a commiserating pity. The hero of *Le Tic* is such a one. His tic is a convulsive reaching with a zigzag motion for something in empty air. The explanation: he had put his daughter in the coffin himself when a temporary short-circuiting of the life signs had caused a physician to pronounce her dead. The voice of the daughter from her grave had delivered a blow to his mind from which he could not recover. Here in mid-career appears that necrophobia of which we have spoken previously and which undermined his battle against insanity.

In September *Un Fou?* was published. Many who have discussed the autobiographical significance of *Le Horla* have chosen to say little about this story. Yet here is perhaps the most worthwhile repository of facts relating to Maupassant's psychological troubles. The wretched hero's death in an insane asylum has a shudderingly significant portent for the reader familiar with Maupassant's own death. The hero's death provides the customary excuse for raising a question as to whether the man had truly been sane, so that insanity may reasonably be noted as the cause of death. Maupassant succeeds remarkably here in leading us back into the life of a man which seems more credible than incredible, and in creating a hero in whom we can believe, despite his grotesquely exaggerated personality.

Can we afterward still consider as absurd his conviction that he was about to be robbed by *another* of his thought? How basic it is to all that we know about man's fears! Is it possible to dismiss the thought that Maupassant was expressing his own experience, and that the *Fou* is but a thinly disguised Guy de Maupassant? This other one (his double) is significantly like that second self who tormented Maupassant into believing someone waited to steal "his thought, that is to say his soul, the soul, that sanctuary, that secret self, the soul, that depth of the individual thought to be impenetrable, the soul, that asylum of unutterable thoughts, of everything one does not permit to be seen of all the secret loves of everything that one wishes to conceal from all other human beings, he opens it, he violates it, displays it, throws it before the public!" (V, 277–78).

The story brings to mind the strange inner world evoked by Dostoevski and Gogol, and suggests further how parallel are the concerns, motifs, and techniques of all the fin de siècle writers. Like Dostoevski's Golyadkin of *The Double*, Jacques Parent has watched himself with morbid, helpless fascination: "One would say that there was someone else imprisoned in me who wished ceaselessly to escape, to act in spite of me, who moved about

restlessly, bit me, exhausted me" (V, 278). Fear of this strange
guest is of the same intensity as that evinced by the hero of *Lui?*
Maupassant had returned to perhaps the most haunting of his
many mental problems. But renewing the study must have given
him little comfort, for the hero's life emerges as strongly reminiscent of the life of Gogol's hero in *Diary of a Madman,* where
the insanity of the hero is evident. The incessant returning to this
sort of material on Maupassant's part, the graphically described
psychological states present a strong case for its autobiographical
ramifications.

Before death released him from his troubles, Maupassant
showed the same marked tendency toward masochism and self-
mutilation as the story's hero, Jacques Parent. The very imagination that could project a scene where a hero bullied his reluctant
dog into a readiness to bite him, only to chase it off at the last
moment, leads one to do some unpleasant speculating. Jacques
Parent becomes convinced that another man is acting for him.
(Sometimes Maupassant saw himself writing his books!) The
story, aside from its probable close connection with Maupassant's
own aberrations, provides a fine literary portrayal of the battle
between the individual and his alter ego. Its author, thereby,
joins a select group of important writers of fiction, many of whom
have been treated with far more respect and given greater place
in literature than critics are willing to accede to Maupassant. The
behavior that marked the last days of Maupassant's life may be
attributed to the alter ego who, as in the case of *Un Fou?* found
at last the light it had sought. The doomed author had an ever-
increasing fear of that being within who would begin to behave
irresponsibly while he watched, helpless to intervene.

VII   *From His Journals*

The year 1885 marks an important moment for the biographer
of Maupassant. His travel journal, *Sur l'Eau,* provides a firsthand
account of what had been his attitudes until then. It is completely
honest. But to understand it one should have an extensive knowledge of his fiction. On occasion it provides the key to understanding his fiction, but more often his fiction provides a critic with
the wherewithal to seize the real import of the entries in the
journal. Its forthrightness will be seen in the following agonized
assessment of his ever-present physical suffering:

The migraine, the horrible evil, the migraine which tortures as no other torture has ever been able to do, which pulverizes the head, drives one crazy, scatters thoughts and disperses memory as dust by the wind, the migraine had latched onto me, and I had to spread out on my bunk with a flask of ether beneath my nostrils. (XXVIII, 98)

How vulnerable were the sensitive fibers of his mind to the possible meaning of these terrible headaches! He had been in the grip of a mortal fear that this was the first sign of approaching insanity from the moment that he had noticed the persistency of the attacks. The fear was now close to reality. His narrative ability became more and more an instrument for telling his own story as he moved closer to the darkness:

My mind follows black valleys which lead me I know not where. They follow one another, intertwine, deep and wide, inescapable. I come out of one merely to enter another, and I do not foresee what will be the end of the last one. I fear that lassitude may cause me later to abandon this fruitless trek. (XXVIII, 99)

Maupassant protests too much. We know his fears when he argues that the use of ether to treat his migraines is really quite harmless. He uses as his comparison the effects of more powerful drugs. No doubt opium would have been worse for him, but the very urgency of telling yourself and others that you know how to use a drug suggests buried doubts about the manner in which you are able to tolerate it. "It wasn't dreamlike as with hashish, they weren't the slightly sickly opium dreams; it was a prodigious sharpness of reason, a new manner of seeing, of judging, of appreciating the things of life, with the certainty, the absolute knowledge that that manner was the true one" (XXVIII, 100).

VIII   *Studies of Criminal Madness*

And the fiction dealing with various types of madness and its provocations continued to enlarge his works along with these autobiographical observations during the year 1885. Quite interesting is Maupassant's gradually evolving attitude toward madness. In September we have another story in whose title we have the word *fou,* but this time he is not ready to call his mad hero's folly anything other than demented: therefore there is no interro-

gation point after the word *fou,* and he precedes it with the in-
definite article, thus—*Un Fou.* At issue are homicidal tendencies.
Maupassant's hero, a judge with power to condemn to death those
who come before him, is clearly insane. We have seen that the
author throughout his life was against those who by reason of
politics held a conventional power, who were able to exercise
influence based upon accepted conventions regardless of their
validity. Perhaps his bitterness against this ever-present fact of
man's society is the final weight causing him to judge his hero as
insane. But for whatever reason, he shows here a willingness to
forgo the usual practice of raising the question: who is insane?
The change here reflects an evolution in his own thinking on the
matter.

Maupassant's use of the diary is one of the characteristics of
his work that puts him in a special category. He kept a sketchy
one himself, and so many of his characters are vulnerable only
as we see them in their diaries. The author was disturbed at
how well his acquaintances, indeed the sophisticated among his
countrymen, wore their masks. The judge's diary reveals his gradual addiction, first to sentencing an accused to death, and then
to being present at the execution. Necrophilism is by now a part
of Maupassant's art and life and reveals itself in many shades for
those attracted to it as a subject for fiction. The mad judge poses
a question that had to be shaped by an author with a mind whose
uncommon quality was not uniquely its artistic powers: "for
isn't killing that which most resembles creating?" (XXI, 162).
Maupassant's ambivalence between necrophobia and necrophilism
is evident. He was not attracted, himself, by the prospect of
homicide—but by self-homicide. His interest in homicide manifests itself and perhaps purges itself of any attraction for it
through the continual treatments of slaughter in his works: the
bitch hound in *Une Vie;* the decrepit jackass in *L'Ane;* the old
horse in *Coco;* and the famous incident recorded in *Sur les Chats*
of the death of a cat, about which we shall later speak. It is quite
easy to make a case for the pathological nature of the hero's sa-
dism. Not so easy for the admirer of Maupassant is it to admit the
pathological character of the author's *intense fascination* with the
workings of the mind of the homicidal maniac, even when we
grant his desire to omit no type of madness in his work.

A madness that leads the judge to justify killing on the grounds

that man's failure to define a "being" reveals the unique clever-
ness inherent in a certain kind of madness. Maupassant was familiar with all types of mad ingenuity and so understood the kind
that could deliver a convincing argument and conclude: "Why,
then, is it a crime to kill? Killing is in our temperament; we must
kill" (*ibid.*). This rationalization possesses that strikingly in-
genious juggling of laws and values to fit a purpose for which
madmen show such a great aptitude. It leads to this conclusion:
"For killing is the great law cast by nature into the mind of the
being. There is nothing more beautiful nor honorable than to
kill" (XXI, 164). Maupassant here is concerned with how men
of genius tainted with madness can, with little difficulty, cast
doubt upon a society's moral code and its values whose unin-
spired conventionality makes them vulnerable. The judge has decided that the laws against killing one's fellow man are predicated upon specious reasoning. The July entries in his diary
show that he now cannot be satisfied by killing with the gavel,
he must himself be the executioner. "Temptation entered into me
like a creeping worm" (XXI, 167).

In the story *Un Fou* Maupassant watches madness spread and
finally engulf his hero, with no idea of offering an apology for it
as had been his intention in many of the previous stories. His
fascination with the rapid growth of the monstrous disease moves
one to somber thoughts about what inspired this change of emphasis: there are strong reasons to conclude that he was already
fearful that soon he would stand helplessly watching an insidious
spreading of the disease from which he knew he was suffering.

The judge first satisfies his craving to kill by cutting the throat
of a pet bird belonging to one of his servants and then watching
as the creature struggles in his blood for life. The episode recalls
one just as macabre, or perhaps more so, which Maupassant recorded in *En Voyage*. He had come upon a group of hysterical
Moslem fanatics who demonstrated their concentration upon
Allah by devouring live lambs, wool, skin, blood and flesh down
to the bare bones. That Maupassant experienced the same horrible thrill as a spectator to this exhibition as the judge to the
death of the bird is of significance.

After the bird only a human sacrifice could satisfy the judge:
first he killed a friendly, most respectful clerk, and then again
and again he killed, more easily each time, more fascinated by

the details of the fear and suffering of the dying. He framed his nephew for a murder he himself had committed, deriving the most exquisite pleasure from the look on the unfortunate young man's face as he sentenced him to the guillotine. No one would believe him when he named himself as the perpetrator of such crimes. What Maupassant suggests is that no one can believe the things that lie in the mind of man, especially the things an exceptional mind contains.

La petite Roque provides us with a careful study of the hallucinations, fears, and mental disintegration of a provincial mayor, Renardet, that is worthy of a clinical psychiatrist. A murderrapist, it is only Renardet who will be responsible for his crime's publication. He cannot stay alone with the burden of his guilt. The repression of what one deems to be "guilty" desires is often responsible for introducing him to a road at the end of which lies insanity. But the mayor does not seek to repress his desire. He acts; however, afterward he cannot live with the remorse his act causes him. Criminal madness still fascinated Maupassant. He seemed interested in studying the psychological verity of Hamlet's remark that "conscience doth make cowards of us all." Conscience suddenly grasps the soul of a man who all of his life has been an example of the crassness of privilege and middle-class power. The discovery that he possesses a conscience surprises him as much as it does the world that regards such men as without conscience. The conscience weighs with fatal consequence upon a brain conditioned only to esteem hedonistic concepts. Madness is the inevitable issue.

Maupassant depicts Renardet's struggle to go on living as before, playing the hypocrite and declaring ironically that he will catch the villain who murdered and raped La Petite Roque. He describes the appearance of the first signs of madness. After a summer of fruitless questioning and searching, the authorities are prepared to drop the case; but Renardet cannot be satisfied to leave the case unsolved because he must *confess and be punished*. His first insane impulse is to obliterate the scene of the crime, thinking thereby some way he may rid himself of the guilt. He sacrifices a valuable timber forest in this effort, standing where a tree might just perchance fall upon him and crush him; but he was only grazed. The only atonement which he can settle upon as equal to the crime is suicide. But he is a coward. And now his madness manifests itself in the elaborate schemes he develops for tricking his cowardice. What were Maupassant's thoughts prior to his own attempt at suicide? An important part of his analysis of Renardet is the effect of loneliness upon his already psychopathic condition: "He suffered from living alone, he suffered both morally and physically from it" (I, 43). It had been this loneliness after the death of his wife that had magnified a vigorous sexual appetite until it had driven him to his brutal act. Maupassant was thinking about his mentor when he had Renardet cry out: "Here I am like Saint Anthony" (I, 44).

Maupassant's heroes never possess the kind of fanatical resolve or dedication that can cause them to walk away from temptation; their madness is never related to their asceticism and abstemiousness; it comes in the aftermath of indulgence in the form of guilt. Again the terrible struggle Maupassant made to shape himself more closely after the master, to be satisfied with the lonely discipline of writing and to reject all distractions of the flesh, is recalled. He studies ordinary man's incapacity for such a life in Renardet, punishing his hero with madness for his failure to exercise the kind of discipline he as a creative writer has forced upon himself and which, ironically, is helping to open the doors of his own mind to insanity. Maupassant was fascinated by madness like a doomed old soldier by engines of death.

Renardet was tempted by the "Vénus rustique" who had inspired Maupassant's first success in the literary field, a fatal enchantress because she was irresistible to the man of the hero's dispositions. In the maddening stillness of his lonely room the mayor is prey to hallucinations in which he is committing the crime over again, and in which she appears in his room and watches him silently. The terrors of the night for the man who is losing his mind have an eerie, moving reality when one realizes that they come from one tragically afflicted himself: "But the night, the impenetrable night, thicker than walls, and empty, the infinite night, so black, so vast, where you can brush against frightful things, the night where you feel mysterious fright wandering, gnawing, seemed to him to be hiding an unknown danger, close by, menacing" (I, 51).

Renardet wrote a confession and posted it. Then cowardice

seized him, and he disgraced himself in an effort to retrieve the
letter from the postman. The latter's refusal finally determined
him to carry out his suicide plan.

IX   *Moving Closer to the Mirror*

Sur les Chats, February, 1886, is an autobiographical fragment.
Here is revealed with no disguise the necrophilism that is trans-
ferred to the characters in many of the stories we have discussed
here. This revelation makes it quite clear that one is meeting
Maupassant in his work more often than not and that a biography
that does not use the man-in-his-works approach will inevitably
be quite incomplete and even, in some cases, tend toward the
specious presentation that ultimately does damage to an artist's
reputation. The episode described in *Sur les Chats* is discussed
often by critics, but many readers of Maupassant do not read the
critics. It reveals a pathological state in the writer, a cruel side
which is not what we like to see, and which we will not forgive
in little boys who drown cats or throw them in liquid cement, as
just a "prank." Maupassant was not, in his sane moments, a cruel
person. That is why discovery of this morbid fascination with pain
and suffering in the child, Guy, tells of the early deviations that
were aggravated by his worsening health until they destroyed him.
A cat, one day, leapt into Maupassant's lap while he was reading:
"I love them and I detest them, these charming and perfidious
animals. . . . The touch of that living robe produced in my fingers
a strange and ferocious desire to strangle the beast I was
caressing" (I, 156–57). And after mentioning this impulse, he
decided that he must study its origins. He then recalled how as
a child he had taken an extreme sadistic pleasure in contem-
plating the death agonies of a cat caught in a snare from which
he could have, at his pleasure, freed the animal: "I watched it
die with palpitating and cruel joy . . ." (I, 158).

Several months later, in the same year, Maupassant was again
considering suicide, its causes, and *the kind of strength* needed
for it. The strong will of the Norman peasant and his dedication
to the rule that sons should obey their fathers are presented as
obstinate furies in his story *Le Père Amable*. An old man whose
son refused to heed his order that he not marry a woman with a
child which would be yet another mouth to feed watches with a
maniacal mixture of satisfaction and anguish as his prediction

that trying to feed that many will kill the son is borne out. And after the death of his son, the intrusion of a new provider into his home is too much for the embittered old peasant. Again old age haunts Maupassant. Here he envisions the frightful hopelessness of its victims caught in a world where none of their ideas or wishes is heeded, where they can make no imprint whatsoever. The old man's solution was suicide. Increasingly, it is noticeable that characters who are strong in their beliefs cannot find a compromise way. It is all or nothing. And that is the way it finally turned out for Maupassant.

In August, 1886, Maupassant had just published *Un Cas de Divorce* in which he returned to the Maupassant we tend to appreciate the most, the one who is angered about the hypocrisy inherent in the promotion of the conventional way of reacting to things. He is out to show up society again as heinous for ostracizing, incarcerating, or branding as mad those who flout its self-perpetuating and valueless conventions. The story in point presents a strongly personal summation of the arguments against marriage Maupassant had offered all along. In addition to this, it reveals quite distinctly a characteristic of Maupassant not heretofore evident, a penchant for decadent tastes. And hence, though we can consider him in many respects as a loner after his break with the Naturalist school, we can at the same time see how similar are his tastes and attitudes to those of the Symbolist-Decadent school. For the hero, Monsieur Chassel, is a dandy. We do not have much biographical evidence of the dandyesque in Maupassant. But here Maupassant is defending the esoteric and eccentric tastes of his hero and poking fun at the lawyer who is using these very oddities as grounds for divorce and who describes them as "pathological." Monsieur Chassel is a Des Esseintes. Maupassant had not forgotten Huysmans nor their conversations during the time when they were both contributing to Zola's "soirées" at Médan.

His pessimism, flowing into the ever-mounting river of his troubles, can be heard in the words of his hero: "How sad and ugly everything is, always the same, always odious" (XXIV, 220). Maupassant deems his creation "poetically mad" because of his revulsion at the oneness of everything. The attitude may explain a certain turn toward the Decadent, dandyesque ideas in Maupassant as well as in his hero; for the latter's complaint expresses the sort of discouragement that Maupassant felt during the last decade of his life: "Always woods, little woods, *rivers which look like rivers, plains which look like plains, all is the same and monotonous*" (italics mine) (*ibid.*). The outburst reveals the evidence that Maupassant was well informed regarding the attitudes of the Decadents, and there is no evidence of parody in the story, all of which suggests that he very well may have shared artistic and philosophic interests in common with the Decadent-Symbolist poets and storytellers. Following the growing conflict between Chassel and his wife leads one again to observe how fixed was Maupassant's idea that connubial bliss is a state not to be attained. His certainty that marriage is always a hoax, then, remained unshaken; and his bitterness in speculating upon how man takes a woman for something ideal *before* marriage is reminiscent of the idea of many a writer during the period of the Decadence—Baudelaire had reached the point where he could no longer consider Madame Sabatier as the ideal. He continued to prefer skepticism and celibacy to risking disillusionment in marriage. And only loneliness and fear of an encounter with that second self ever threatened to undermine his obstinate opposition to it.

Here Maupassant causes his hero to "run the risk" so that he finds the bitter disillusion: "Now she's my wife. So long as I desired her ideally she was for me the unrealizable dream about to be realized. Beginning with the very second I held her in my arms she was no longer anything but the being nature had used in order to deceive all of my hopes" (XXIX, 223).

It is at this point that Chassel's attitude reveals a state of mind that a biographer must puzzle over. Should it be regarded as having no relation whatever to the strange and troubled mental activities of its creator? At this time in Maupassant's life he had already written a great many stories which biographers have regarded as mirrorings of the progress of his madness. The confession of Chassel seems very likely to provide another important reflection: he tells of his utter disgust with the bestiality of human sex and of his admiration for the purity of flowers which "reproduce, they, they alone, in the world without blight upon their inviolable race" (XXIV, 225). Over and over we have noted and shall note further Maupassant's aversion to the manner in which men cover over "bestiality" with the blessing of the Church and

"God." That he regarded sex in this manner reveals a strange and fanatically puritanistic strain that stuck with him throughout his life and which can be traced from one end to the other in his works, despite his numerous efforts to paint himself as a most irreverent and uninhibited debunker of sexual morality. His hatred of the Church-sanctioned marriage rested not upon any inherent religious intolerance but rather upon what he deemed as its effort to camouflage something *he regarded* as essentially bestial. He did not go quite as far as his mad hero, Chassel, in cultivating a "flower harem"; but the very imagination which invented the idea and created the doting caretaker with his algolagnic pain and joy at the death of a flower shows some strange but familiar strains of the madness of the Decadence itself. The lawyer's plea for a ruling in Madame Chassel's favor is substantiated with the argument that such behavior is insane.

The story is interesting because it has that unique, startling quality that the best of the Decadents were capable of producing. And it shows clearly how Maupassant was linked to the Decadents, indeed how Naturalism, the Decadence, and Symbolism were all three commonly related. This page of Maupassant's literary career is scarcely ever turned by biographers.

The obsessive fear of being alone which Maupassant shared with so many of his characters had its origins, as we have often noted, in the fear that the infernal being within would never permit him to be alone. If it was not a confrontation with this inner being, loneliness would produce fears which in turn would become hallucinations. In 1886 *L'Auberge* tells of the terrors of one of two caretakers of an Alpine lodge when, during their yearly lonely vigil in the winter-isolated inn, his companion goes out in a storm and never returns. Alone, the younger of the two imagines he hears the ghost of the old man wailing outside the cabin. He loses control and barricades himself against the invasion of the soul of his frozen partner. He soon depletes the stock of strong drink and can no longer deaden the sounds of weeping and scratching he hears at the door. In spring the owners return. Before the door lies the skeleton of a dog. The door must be broken in and behind it there is a madman: "a man with white hair which fell to his shoulders, a beard that tumbled down to his chest, glittering eyes and tatters hanging over his body" (V, 221).

X *Toward a Masterpiece of Terror and Madness*

The lonely man had become a constant source of fiction for Maupassant. That was in part due to the increase in his own loneliness. There were no more Flauberts. The relationship with his mother was fraught with nagging financial problems, with the petty trivia of all but the rarest of such relationships, and with his overindulgent concern for her health which quickened the progress of the malady in his own overburdened, overworked, and highly sensitive brain. He had always been so different from his brother, Hervé, that no one would have supposed they were brothers. But now he feared more and more that what had befallen his brother was dreadfully near to him. And these unsoothing circumstances were rendered virulent by the fact that there was nowhere for a man like Maupassant to turn except into himself. The world of the introvert was not a natural one for him. We have seen how he hated it as a young man and how he had rebelled against its confinements. And now he was forced into it, to the very heart of the one abiding fear of his life, loneliness. It was almost inevitable that this strange person he did not want to meet, the other Maupassant, would be thrust upon him.

And thus we find that in 1886 Maupassant had reached the point where he could no longer doubt that he was talking about himself when he spoke of the madmen and their hallucinations. It was the year in which he fashioned what most consider to be his masterpiece among the stories of terror and madness, *Le Horla*. His biography flashes forth even in allusions to objects: the house stirs acute memories of Flaubert's from which Maupassant had often seen what he has his hero see: "From my windows I see the Seine which is flowing along my garden, behind the road, nearly in my yard, the long and wide Seine which goes from Rouen to Havre, covered with ships passing" (V, 3–4). The hero's symptomatic *"tristesse"* resembles very closely what Maupassant was experiencing at the time. That this state is the foreboding of a calamitous mental disorder ready to materialize in the story suggests a parallel suspicion that his own *tristesse* was the foreboding of something calamitous in his own life. The hero, like his creator, refuses to believe that this vague malaise isn't something to be forgotten in work. What the mind did to him was just what the highly imaginative mind of Guy de Maupassant was doing to him. "Decidedly, I'm ill. And a month ago I was fine!" (V, 6). Insomnia, which doubtless held back the healing forces of oblivion that Maupassant needed, keeps the hero in a frightful state of expectation. The diary might very well be identical to one Maupassant didn't keep or which we haven't been able to find. That is the opinion of a number of biographers who take its revelations as pertaining more than obliquely to the author himself: "No change! My state is truly bizarre . . . fear of sleep and fear of the bed . . . someone draws near me, looks at me, runs his hands over me, takes my throat in his hands and squeezes . . . squeezes . . . with all his strength in an effort to strangle me" (V, 8).

July is marked by the jubilant assurance that a flight to Saint-Michel has shaken the mysterious malady which has been stalking him. Maupassant was, himself, constantly deluding himself during the last years that being on the go, that furious efforts to find peace, would somehow outrace the fury bearing down upon him. Like the hero of *Le Horla*, a return to familiar surroundings etched the brutal certainty upon his mind that there was for him no lasting peace, no escape. Here we see demonstrated the validity of the assertion of numerous Maupassant critics that he suffers with his characters; for here his own suffering is the work's substance. Poignant is the presentation of the disillusion of all of those who believe in the miracle of partings and voyages, because it is the result of the experience of a man who had found all the wells along the route of a journey toward peace dry, and who had to turn homeward for the bitter water of reality. He made the journey more frequently than most have. When the hero cries out "I am becoming mad," one perceives more accurately the width of the chasm between the sane and the insane. There is nothing to be done but to watch the progress of madness in the victim, though one would prefer to arrest it. The tension and extreme awareness of one's impotence in the dreadful spectacle are certainly in part due to one's knowledge that Maupassant died a madman. The biographer can do nothing, of course, except to show how even out of the tragic years of decline the artist drew something of value and lasting beauty which would not have been the same had he not been so cruelly twisted by fate.

The effect of solitude is described in the victim's diary in words strikingly similar to those we find in Maupassant's own diary, *La Vie Errante:*

> The people form a stupid herd, one time idiotically patient and another ferociously revolting. Someone tells them: "Have a good time!" They have a good time. Then they say: "Go and fight your neighbor." They fight. They are commanded: "Vote for the Emperor." They vote for the Emperor.
>
> Those who direct the herd are just as stupid; but instead of obeying men, they obey principles, which can be nothing but stupid, sterile, and false, by the very fact that they are principles, that is to say respected, certain, unchangeable ideas in a world where no one is sure of anything.... (V, 18–19)

How could a man who felt this way be happy and not be alone, or be happy when he was alone? The few to whom Maupassant could turn had diminished as the years had passed. He was not so entirely without worthwhile companionship, as was his hero. But the deepening of his troubled state and of his antipathy only served to isolate him.

August's entry tells of a madness moving at a gallop pace: now the hero no longer thinks there is a difference between reality and hallucination; all that exists truly for him is the product of his mental state. And so the hope that once had made him capable of looking upon the notion that he was being possessed by some evil power as nonsense no longer prevailed. His certainty of the fact made him believe that the stems of roses were broken before his eyes: "The flower arose, following the arc that an arm bearing it toward a mouth would have taken. . ." (V, 28). There was nothing but air when he reached out. And water was drunk from the decanter beside his bed under his conviction of possession, as certain a fact to him as if it were really so. The fear that this being would appear which had early been responsible for his mental strain is replaced by the opposite fear—that the being would *refuse* to manifest itself, a very special torment. He is mad now. *He knows* the visitor is there. "Someone possesses my soul and governs it" (V, 32). To prove he is not in its power the victim acts with a crazed irresponsibility that he regards as manifesting independence. The efforts not only prove the opposite to the reader but to the hero himself. Maupassant's description of the man possessed is reminiscent of the demonism which is often prominently displayed in the New Testament.

Maupassant had won in his struggle to be independent of the demon who called him to the carefree life. But it was a costly victory, for the calling to the physical world had suited his natural bent, and to refuse it had required a mind-disturbing distortion of his natural propensities. The victory had its sweet aspects: he could see that by defeating the tempter he had made possible his rather large literary accomplishments. He was so certain he had done the right thing, so certain of himself as an artist, almost megalomaniacal in his last years, that he feared his enemy would take some other form in order to strike elsewhere. The new demon he imagined was like the one who tormented the hero of *Le Horla*, there, surely, but refusing to show his face, to play his hand. He feared, as did his creation, that this time the demon would not be thwarted in his plan to destroy him. His fears were well grounded as we all know. Madness kept up its patient, omnipotent pursuit until the human being pursued could go on no farther.

Thus, the fears of the hero of *Le Horla*, exaggerated though they seemed at first, proved well founded. It must have been with considerable horror that Maupassant showed this to be so. His ability to make his hero's battle against Le Horla into a situation with which the reader can identify is the product of his peculiar personal expertise and experience with the furious demons whose shapes and substances are totally unknown to the sane man. One can never be certain as to the degree of closeness of this description of the progress of madness in the hero of *Le Horla* to the progress of the malady in Maupassant, but one can be certain that it is closer than the author himself would have liked to believe. If it is not a completely accurate account, then, it is as close as a biographer will ever come to a reasonable image of Maupassant's case.

The phobias that led Maupassant later to autoscopic hallucinations, his pessimism about mankind's capacity to deal with the present with its portent of a devastating end to the race, and his loneliness are all parts of the story. "My chair was empty, or seemed so; but I understood that he was there, that one, seated in my place, and that he was reading" (V, 36). (This is scarcely a step removed from seeing *himself* there in the chair.) Maybe beings from another world would conquer man. (Such a statement reveals the fatal weakness Maupassant read into man's character when he saw how willingly he became enslaved by conventions.) The plans of the lonely, friendless man to ensnare his invisible tormentor resemble Maupassant's lonely plans to make a "comeback" with *L'Angélus*. As if he needed a comeback! But he was so sure, near the end, that he had been forsaken, that his works were not receiving their due, that there was a plot to belittle and downgrade him, and that if he didn't complete this work he would be proven to be the madman his enemies were calling him. He had enemies as does every man of talent or position, but his illness caused him to magnify them out of all reasonable proportion, so that he forgot that calumny and belittling and personal invective are sores upon which frustrated little men always feed and upon which sometimes frustrated big men feed; he decided that it had all been initiated for his misery and destruction. The stark cry of despair that breaks from the madman's lips at the end of *Le Horla* is one of the most moving pronouncements of surrender to be found in Maupassant's work. The moment the author himself realized there was no hope of evicting the possessor, he must have felt, thought, uttered words with something of the same import: "No . . . No . . . without any doubt, but the slightest . . . it is not dead. . . . Therefore . . . therefore . . . it is going to be necessary for me to kill myself!" (V, 48). Can one ever forget the picture of Maupassant, razor in hand, with his throat slashed?

XI *The Unrelenting Furies*

La Vie Errante published in March, 1887, reveals the author's active interest at the time in the causal factors of madness. In this prolonged search, he seemed to seek out what was alien to his own symptoms in an effort to allay his fears. Mention has been made of his determination to keep the danger of addiction to ether at a minimum because of his realization that a total dependence on it as a medication for his migraines might lead to addiction and hence to experimentation with some new drug. He was quick to record in his journal the observation that the madmen in a certain asylum had gotten there through drug addiction:

"Like most of his companions, it was hashish or rather kif which had put him in that state. He's quite young, very pale, very thin, and he talks to me with enormous, troubled, staring eyes" (III, 161). But as he watched these unfortunates go through their strange capers, he had the sickening feeling that the germ of their disease was being transmitted to him: "And one fancies he feels a breath of madness penetrating his soul, a terrifying and contagious emanation of that maleficent insanity" (III, 163). His pity for them and their fascination for him are fraught with irony.

La Nuit of June, 1887, provides further disturbing evidence of the manner in which hallucination and madness had begun to dominate Maupassant's work. His imagination seemed to have come under a tyrannical influence which kept it constantly creating ever more incredible fantasies. For the admirer of Maupassant these pieces, with their grotesque exaggerations, seem efforts at inventing mental situations more desperate than his own; and they emphasize the discouraging, private world of Maupassant during his last years.

"I had never seen Paris so dead, so deserted," announces the story's ever-present narrator (XX, 224). Even Les Halles was deserted, a situation whose eeriness poisoned his fear-prone, madness-prone mind. It is Maupassant's own exaggerated sense of alienation and loneliness that comes out of the mouth of his narrator: "What's happening? Oh, my God! what's happening?" (XX, 227). The author describes his beloved Seine, the presence to which he had always turned in his worst moments at the Ministry, as flowing with the cold silence of death. The terrifying atmosphere of *La Nuit* is the final product of the writer's long season of brooding upon loneliness and death. It is a very strange fact that the night to Maupassant never quite meant the same as to other poets and writers. Rarely does one find it as a source of consolation to him, as a time for peaceful reflection, as the time of a productive solitude. So pervasive was his instinctive fear of night that even when he did enter with enthused awe into the spirit of poetry upon its arrival, the passage would still end up darkly tainted with foreboding. Night was his enemy; its silence provided a solitary path down which he, in spite of himself, would seek himself out, allowing his imagination to run free, and then being afraid of the multifariously cruel splendor of the image of himself it evoked.

Pierre et Jean (1888) offers clear evidence of how his disease and his troubled thoughts about it kept him in a state of turmoil particularly harmful to one of his nervous disposition. The novel makes the sensitive reader aware of the fact that Maupassant was becoming disenchanted even with the things which he had loved the most and upon which he had relied heavily to keep him in a stable frame of mind. The sea, the beach with its lovers whose free and natural behavior had kept alive the hope that there was, after all, a certain undiluted goodness in life; such sources of past assurance seemed to have become transformed into forces for inspiring a degeneration in him now—not a regeneration.

Pierre's reaction to the Trouville Beach sounds this alarming new note. And Pierre shares more than enough of the ideas and attitudes of his creator to suggest that he is, if not the author's double, at least strikingly like him in mentality. It is, then, no wild speculating that leads a biographer to seek to understand Maupassant's negative attitude, in later years, to the things he had formerly loved the most by studying the same phenomenon in Pierre as he roams the areas that had been dear to his thoughts: "From a distance, it [the beach] resembled a long garden filled with dazzling flowers" (XI, 122). But closer examination dispels this rather lovely image of it, revealing one that is rendered unlovely by a pessimism and cynicism regarding man's loves and his ambitions. It is as if, in this drawing near to the beach on the part of Pierre, Maupassant wished to give a rapid view of what his attitude had been at first and how it had now become so completely incapable of arousing his old enthusiasm and positive thinking. "But suddenly, as if he had been jolted awake, he saw them distinctly; and a hatred against them surged up in him, for they seemed happy and content" (XI, 123). Maupassant's work had always rung with a moralizing invective against the people whom he saw as accepting the chains of convention as if they were garlands with a servile, senseless contentment. It is little wonder that by 1888 this, coupled with the many frustrations related to his declining health, caused him to put these harshly cynical words into the mouth of Pierre. The turn about in attitude is complete: "That vast beach, then, was nothing but a love market where some sold, others gave, the latter haggling over their caresses and the former simply sealing the bargain" (XI, 124). Sadly we see Maupassant's systematic rejection of all the things which had formerly given him hope. We are witnesses to the beginning of the final decline toward a loss of *all reasonable perspective*.

Another of the furies that kept in pursuit of Maupassant was that old demon, old age, fashioned by his imagination into a starkly real shade. Maupassant was always acutely aware of the passing of time. Indeed, his awareness of the phenomenon caused him to feel its heavy hand at a time in his life not usually associated with such speculations. He helped old age along by imagining it had already arrived. By 1889 he must have had a premonition that death was near. The desperation with which men seek to conserve their youth is again treated in *Le Masque*, and Maupassant seems bent here upon revealing how absurd it is for men to seek a means of convincing themselves of their immunity to the inevitable. And yet he ends up by underlining his very own inability to face the inevitable which evidenced itself through incapacity to be realistic about such things as his literary reputation, the certainty of his diminishing creative prowess, and his declining health. His failure to face these things resolutely and to accept them for what they were had a great deal to do with the rapidity with which madness engulfed him.

The fall of 1889 saw the publication of *L'Endormeuse*, another frightful bit of evidence to indicate how frequently his thoughts strayed to suicide. That, after torturing his mind with all of its possibilities and its shortcomings, he was still unable to abandon it as a subject for his stories is indication enough of the torment his last years visited upon him. Moreover, there is surely a great deal of significance in the fact that he almost always ended by extending his understanding to the victim whenever it was not his purpose simply to defend suicide as "a most reasonable response" to the conditions that life imposes upon the sensitive soul. These factors seem to indicate that there is much more than a remote connection between the suicide victims of his work and the man who created them. For Maupassant is but giving artistic expression to the very real kinship he felt with these characters. Witness the depth of understanding of their reasons for acting with such finality:

How well I understand them, those who, feeble, harassed by misfortune, having lost loved ones, awakened from the dream about a last-minute reward, from the illusion about another existence where God would finally be just after having been ferocious.

Suicide! Why it's the very strength of those who no longer have any, it's the hope of those who no longer believe, it's the sublime courage of the vanquished. (XIX, 236)

The story, told by the usual narrator, describes a suicide club. Maupassant cannot be said to have been sold on the idea, for his narrator is not. But after being privileged to sniff the gas used for the self-exterminations, the latter is forced to agree that the members offer a most intelligent and pleasant means of self-destruction to any who feel, as they, that suicide is the only way. Such favorable turns in attitude on Maupassant's part are of interest to the one who tries to examine his unsuccessful suicide attempt.

XII *A Crucial Year*

The year 1890 seems to be the crucial year. It marks the beginning of the end. In February appeared a story that justifies the conclusion that by some great personal effort and by a kind stroke of fate much of Maupassant's dwindling powers momentarily returned. If we saw such a rejuvenation in a contemporary author who had been the victim of a disease as dreadful as was Maupassant's, we would surely take it as a sign that our fears had been exaggerated, that he had recovered. Unfortunately, if anyone among his contemporaries was so impressed, he was wrong. *Le Champ d'Oliviers* is very definitely one of his masterpieces. But it is a strange turnabout from the almost fanatical conviction that had marked his earlier writing where he had blamed the warring between fathers and sons on the fathers. And strange turnabouts are what we see in so many of the later works we today still consider to be first rate.

It seems that, in later years, when he tried to return to the old line, he never got beyond a splendid and promising introduction. *L'Angélus* with its great promise was never achieved. There was no longer evident in Maupassant that firm conviction of former times. Almost unquestionably the disease affecting him was partially responsible for this change in attitude. *Le Champ d'Oliviers* deals with a man whose fanatic dedication to a life of piety is nothing short of madness. The instability of his resolve becomes evident with the arrival of an ingrate son. His faith breaks down, his peace is shattered, and he becomes again the violent man he had sought to flee in religious adoration and meditation. It is strange to find Maupassant sympathizing with a father and understanding his suffering—even to find him *admitting* the suffering of fathers. Certainly this change in attitude as reflected in the story would provide some support to Artine Artinian's argument that an affection for his father is evident in the author's latter days: "That affection, far from slackening with time, only became more fortified. . . ."[5] The assertion, however, remains highly debatable.

Maupassant's hero, the Baron de Vilbois, had been driven into the holy life by a capricious woman, a sort of "femme fatale." She had brought disorder into his orderly daily routine and madness into his mind. (Her kinship to Nana suggests the author's connection to the Naturalists in general and to Zola in particular.) He had married her, and she, performing as so many of Maupassant's women did, had cuckolded him. (We notice another turnabout: Maupassant had lost interest in justifying cuckoldry.) Vilbois was aware that his wife was sleeping with his best friend; and she gloried in flaunting her infidelity before him:

But she, child of the sidewalks of Paris, as impudent as she was lewd, sure of the next man as the one right now, moreover bold like those daughters of the people who mount the barricades by simple gameness, stands up to him and insults him; and when he draws back his fist, she shows him she's pregnant. (XXIV, 51–52)

Driven insane by her fatal tantalizing, he would have killed her when she told him it was the other man's child she was going to bear. But, instead, he broke with her and became a monk. No longer whole mentally, he was hiding from woman in the church, prompted by maniacal fears of her power to destroy man. Misogyny became a cult.

The appearance of his son, armed with a portrait of Vilbois himself, which proved his wife had lied to him, that the unborn child had been his, opened the old wounds. He realized that fate had no intention of allowing him to live in the sweet oblivion he had found as a priest. All of the violence in his character which he had carefully walled up by patient discipline and faith broke forth. Madness engulfed him again. But momentarily the sight of his own son did touch him. The moment passed, and the young visage under the influence of too much drink took on a hellish resemblance to that of his mother. The sight of those well-remembered and long-feared traits resurrected the fury that had lain so still in his heart that Vilbois had mistakenly thought it dead. His anger mounted as he listened to the young man relate boastfully how he had attacked his rich politician stepfather who had refused to humor him after his wife's death. The son had just been released from prison and had come in hopes of using his real father as his mother had once done.

The reminder of his unfaithful wife and the presence of this nasty, insolent son were too much for the priest. He saw to it that the young man passed out from drink. Then he arranged the room as if a great struggle had taken place. This done, he committed suicide. When the villagers summoned by the good woman who did the monk's cooking and house chores found them, there was little way that the besotted young man could prove he hadn't murdered the good priest. With all of its strange reversals in attitude, the story presents as its protagonist a man who resembles many of those in his later stories: for him things had become so bad that self-destruction was the only means of escaping madness, the only removal from what he deemed the madness around him.

Qui Sait? is the last of the stories that seems clearly tied to Maupassant's rapidly deteriorating mental health. It is another product of the crucial year, 1890, but a bit over three years prior to his death at the asylum of Dr. Blanche. The setting is terrifyingly familiar to one who has watched the progress of Maupassant's life flash past him on the horizon of the author's work: again we are led into the ward of a mental institution. Here it is the central character himself who asks our indulgence in listening to his story and judging his sanity. He assures us that he is not like the others, that his presence here is voluntary, that he only entered so as not to be alone with himself in an environment where the hallucinations to which he was prey would more surely be encouraged to run their course. The recurrence in the work of Maupassant of this identical figure with the same explanations for his behavior forces one to the appalling conclusion that it is neither lack of imagination nor sterility that is responsible for these repetitions but the fact that the author was unable to avoid speaking of a condition which had now closed in on him so tightly as to scarcely permit him to exercise his mind outside of it or see beyond it.

The hero describes an early life whose condition is uncomfortably close to the Maupassant condition. He had been a dreamer. Initially he had harbored no bitterness against God or his fellow man. But then he had discovered how boring and unimaginative were the people, and the knowledge had made him remove himself from them by progressive steps until now he could no longer tolerate their presence. He had come to hate Paris because it was a place whose entire being was nourished by mediocrity and by the illusion that the world of extroversion was of necessity the best of all possible worlds. His loathing for the literary salons with their pseudo-philosophers and poets duplicates Maupassant's sentiments in later life as does his decision that he must bend his efforts to the creation of a setting in which *he* can live and think. Maupassant had done exactly this with his hermitage, "La Guillette." Though it is the hero of *Qui Sait?* speaking in the following, there can be little doubt that the ideas expressed are autobiographical: "my house became, had become, a world where I lived a solitary and active life, in the midst of objects, furnishings, familiar curios, friendly to my gaze like friendly faces" (XXIV, 236). (We have previously seen how the yacht *Bel-Ami* also had provided Maupassant a world of familiar furnishings where he could live "a solitary and active life.")

The yearning to be hidden on the part of the hero of *Qui Sait?* is another detail which coincides with Maupassant's contradictory behavior of later life, when abandoning his former proclivity for playing the exhibitionist he went to the other extreme and sought a world behind curtains. And it was not because he hated the publicity that fame bestows! For ironically, Maupassant never tired of attempting to inspire awe among the very people whose taste and ignorance he openly abhorred.

Maupassant certainly did not leave his carefully planned and constructed retreat and return to find it as completely different as did his hero in *Qui Sait?* But it is probable that the story is a monstrous exaggeration of some significant change he himself imagined when he was having one of his worst nights. Merely the hero's suspicion that something fatal had happened at his retreat during his short absence was enough to unbalance him so that he surrendered to a conglomerate of fears and hallucinations which he would once have probed until they rendered up a logical explanation. The surrender marked his crossing the narrow corridor separating genius from madness: he was no longer able to keep a rein on his imagination, to put it to any constructive purpose. He had become its victim; and Maupassant's imagination of what occurs when one's imaginative genius turns upon him is indeed an illumination of considerable dimensions. "And there, suddenly I saw, on my doorsill, an armchair, my big reading chair, waddling forth from my house" (XXIV, 242). He darted madly to and fro in an attempt to stop this mad exodus of all of his furnishings. The next day he deemed his servant paid him a visit to inform him of the astonishing exodus. It was surely a theft that had occurred. For the months following he resembled Gogol's wretched little functionary whose life was turned into a madness of lamentations and beseechings poured out on the deaf ears of peers and gods because of the theft of an overcoat. Like his creator, the hero allowed himself to be deluded into the belief that a voyage could stem the terrible tide of his mental illness; and also like him he came back convinced of the cure until he again set foot on the soil where his madness had been born and thrived. Maupassant was very blunt in the manner in which he rejected the idea that there is any escape, any *re-creation* possible. Once one of his characters had come inevitably back to the country that had produced him, like himself, he found the old disillusions and disappointments, the matrix of madness, awaiting. "Mercy! What a shock! One of my beautiful wardrobes was there at the end of an archway filled with different things" (XXIV, 248). Coming back to Rouen must have caused Maupassant to find the ghosts he had fled on his voyages as surely as his mad hero's return to that city caused him to stumble upon his past.

The madman's effort to catch the merchant from whom he had purchased a piece of his own furniture came to no avail. He brought the police, and neither the merchant nor the furniture was there. His servant informed him that all the furniture had been returned. But it would never serve him again, for he was shut away in a madhouse where he whined pitifully about the possibility that the merchant whom he blamed for his madness might be shut up in the same room with him.

We have now seen how Maupassant managed his inordinate

fears of solitude, of old age, and of death. He avoided giving over to them entirely for a remarkably long time, especially considering that the physical and mental maladies which beset him weakened him to such a considerable degree. He mastered them in large part by studying their effects on his imaginative creations, by occupying himself with the large and somewhat idealistic task of articulating what few people had known or understood about madness. The articulation acted as a pressure valve: he released sufficiently his fears to purge himself of enough of the deadly poison to delay his own destruction. But the continual buildup of what remained of the poison got him in the end. The extreme difficulty of the task of discussing the unknown without resorting to the superstitions and hocus-pocus characteristic of ghost stories or the sensational violence associated with so many of the ordinary stories about madness was another factor which challenged his mind to the point that it would not let itself be undermined early by the forces working toward its ultimate destruction.

XIII   *Conclusion*

Though the many works discussed quite obviously had much to do with the longevity of Maupassant's struggling against the inevitable conqueror, they contain for us much hard evidence concerning the progress of the madness that finally killed him. Its patient evil progress and his struggle to contain if not destroy it is a dramatic story which—if Maupassant did not wish to tell it, and he certainly didn't wish to do so—he tells to the patient critic of his work. We have seen how the events of Maupassant's life, though by no means an encouraging or favorable array, each separately inspired some of his finest pages. Certainly this is nowhere truer than in the case of his mental suffering. One is compelled to suggest, though with sadness, that had not madness been the persistent worm it was in his life, we would be very much the losers. Even the work that does not deal with what is normally considered to be pathological behavior would have been far less intense and hence less convincing.

As is true of all such voluminous collections, there are a few items we would be just as well off without. But this takes nothing away from the fact that Guy de Maupassant has fashioned for himself a place in the forefront of the world's short-story writers.

Like so many great personalities, he failed in establishing his greatness in areas he considered to be the most important of all. Time has not shown that those who ignored his importance as a novelist erred greatly. And his achievements in lyric poetry and the theater are so meagre as to warrant little serious study. No matter what one can find to take away, however, there remains much which bears the stamp of a master.

Maupassant's biography will always remain a little less substantial than the biographies of most illustrious men. The complete record that forms a convincing base for so many biographies does not exist in the case of Maupassant. The reasons for this seem obvious: it was too painful for Laure de Maupassant to share all about her famous son with the world; and, at the other end of the spectrum, he provided too tempting a target for caricaturists and those like the Goncourts whose colorings of him are suspect because of a certain enmity they bore toward him. The lines are, thus, too distinctly drawn for us to rely upon the evidence presented by either side as representing the full story. Where the anecdotal has replaced the true is a matter of conjecture. The one sure source is his work. There is always the danger that one will be mistaken in some of his assumptions when he has to rely so heavily upon the creative work of an author to furnish answers to the questions that an incomplete biography raises. But one must run the risk in Maupassant's case. What can be satisfactorily substantiated by this technique seems to outweigh by far the distortions caused by the fallacious assumptions. Maupassant, from the beginning of his career, insisted that he be judged on what he had done, that critics look directly at his work instead of filtering their gaze through their own treatises on what he ought to be doing. It seems that Maupassant may have been giving his future biographers a hint as to how best they might proceed to discover the man behind the far too sketchy and controversial biographical evidence. The more directly we look at his work the closer the image of Guy de Maupassant comes to becoming a distinct totality.

Notes and References

Chapter 2

1. Cuckoldry is treated with varying intensity: *Le Testament, Une Ruse, M. Jocaste, Fort Comme la Mort, Une Répétition* (a one-act drama), *Clair de Lune, Le Vengeur, Fini, Cri d'Alarme, Etrennes, Mont-Oriol, L'Ordonnance, Le Lapin, Nos Lettres, L'Epreuve, Monsieur Parent, La Chambre, Le Petit, Adieu Souvenir, Lui?, Le Mal d'André, Le Cas de Madame Luneau, Un Sage, Décoré!, Monsieur Parent, Les Bécasses, Un Echec, Au Bord du Lit, L'Héritage, L'Assassin, La Revanche, Saunée, Madame Parisse, Pierre et Jean.*

Chapter 6

1. Edouard Maynial, *La Vie et l'oeuvre de Guy de Maupassant* (Paris: Mercure de France, 1906), p. 233.
2. *Ibid.,* p. 236.
3. *Ibid.,* p. 239.
4. *Ibid.,* p. 244.
5. Artine Artinian, ed., *Correspondance Inédite de Guy de Maupassant* (Paris: Editions Dominique Wapler, 1951), p. 47.

Selected Bibliography

PRIMARY SOURCES

Maupassant, Guy de. *Oeuvres complètes.* Paris: Louis Conard, 1925–1947.

1. Novels

Une Vie. Vol. II. 1924.
Bel-Ami. Vol. VII. 1928.
Pierre et Jean. Vol. XI. 1929.
Notre Coeur. Vol. XII. 1929.
Fort comme la Mort. Vol. XIV. 1929.
L'Angélus. (Unfinished.) Vol. XVII. 1930.
Mont-Oriol. Vol. XVIII. 1931.

2. Poetry

Des Vers. Poésies inédites. Vol. VI. 1928.

3. Short Stories

La petite Roque. La Peur. Les Caresses. Vol. I. 1925.
Boule de Suif. Vol. IV. 1926.
Le Horla. Le voyage du Horla. Un Fou? Le Horla (version première). Vol. V. 1927.
Contes de la Bécasse. La Tombe. Vol. VIII. 1928.
Mlle Fifi. M. Jocaste. Vol. X. 1929.
La Maison Tellier. Ma Femme. Les Conseils d'une grand'mère. Vol. XIII. 1929.
(Oeuvres posthumes.) *Le Père Milon, Le Colporteur.* Vol. XVI. 1929.
(Oeuvres posthumes.) *Les Dimanches d'un bourgeois de Paris. La vie d'un paysagiste. L'Ame étrangère.* Vol. XVII. 1930.
La main gauche. L'Endormeuse. Mme Hermet. Vol. XIX. 1932.
Clair de lune. L'Enfant. En Voyage. Le Bûcher. Vol. XX. 1931.

151

Monsieur Parent. Vol. XXI. 1931.
Miss Harriet. Un Million. Vol. XXII. 1947.
Yvette. Misti. Vol. XXIII. 1947.
L'Inutile Beauté. Alexandre. Vol. XXIV. 1947.
Le Rosier de Madame Husson. Souvenirs. Celles qui osent. Vol. XXV. 1947.
Les Soeurs Rondoli. Le Baiser, Vol. XXVI. 1947.
Contes du jour et de la nuit. Humble Drame. Vol. XXVII. 1947.
Toine. Le Père Judas. Vol. XXIX. 1947.

4. Theatre

Théâtre. Une Répétition. Histoire du vieux temps. Mussotte. La Paix du Ménage. Vol. XV. 1930.

5. Essays

Etude sur Gustave Flaubert. Etude sur Emile Zola. Vol. XVII. 1930.

6. Correspondence

Correspondance. Vol. IV. 1926.
Correspondance inédite de Guy de Maupassant. Ed. Artine Artinian with Edouard Maynial. Paris: Dominique Wapler, 1951.
Lettres de Guy de Maupassant à Gustave Flaubert. Ed. Pierre Borel. Avignon: Aubanel, 1941.

7. Journals and Travel Essays

La Vie Errante. Vol. III. 1926.
Notes d'un Voyageur. Vol. VIII. 1928.
Au soleil. La partie de Colomba. Le Monastère de Corbara. Les Bandits Corses. Une Page d'histoire inédite. Vol. IX. 1928.
Sur l'Eau. Blanc et bleu. Livre du Bord. Vol. XXVIII. 1947.

8. Translations

The Works. New York: National Library Company. 1909.
Vol. 1. *Boule de Suif,* and other stories.
Vol. 2. *Monsieur Parent,* and other stories.
Vol. 3. *The Viaticum,* and other stories.
Vol. 4. *The Old Maid,* and other stories.
Vol. 5. *Une Vie,* and other stories.
Vol. 6. *Bel-Ami,* and other stories.

Vol. 7. *Mont-Oriol,* and other stories.
Vol. 8. *Pierre et Jean,* and other stories.
Vol. 9. *Fort comme la Mort,* and other stories.
Vol. 10. *Notre Coeur,* and other stories.

SECONDARY SOURCES

1. Books

ARTINIAN, ARTINE. *Maupassant Criticism in France, 1800–1940.* New York: King's Crown Press, 1941. An essential bibliography.
———. *Pour et contre Maupassant.* Paris: Librairie Nizet, 1955. Interesting, often illuminating opinions of other writers.
BRUNETIÈRE, FERDINAND. *Le Roman naturaliste.* Paris: Calmann-Lévy, 1883. A seminal study on Naturalism with an important if somewhat debatable discussion of Maupassant's place in the movement.
DUMESNIL, RENÉ. *Guy de Maupassant.* Paris: Tallandier, 1947. One of the most original and perceptive studies of Maupassant.
GONCOURT, EDMOND ET JULES. *Journal.* Paris: Flammarion et Fasquelle, n.d. Extremely biased.
LUMBROSO, A. *Souvenirs sur Maupassant.* Rome: Bocca, 1905. Anecdotal but fascinating.
MAYNIAL, EDOUARD. *La Vie et l'oeuvre de Guy de Maupassant.* Paris: Mercure de France, 1906. The base for any study of Maupassant's life as reflected by his work.
MORAND, PAUL. *Vie de Guy de Maupassant.* Paris: Flammarion, 1942. A most readable and impressive biography.
SCHMIDT, ALBERT-MARIE. *Maupassant par lui-même.* Paris: Editions du Seuil, 1965. Very sensitive study of author's life and work.
STEEGMULLER, FRANCIS. *A Lion in the Path.* New York: Random House, 1949. A fine synthesis of the Maupassant studies, both dramatic and scholarly: a valuable collection of the stories attributed to Maupassant which do not appear in the *Oeuvres complètes* is appended.
SULLIVAN, EDWARD. *Maupassant the Novelist.* Princeton, N.J.: Princeton University Press, 1945. A thorough exploration and evaluation of the Maupassant novels.
TASSART, FRANÇOIS. *Souvenirs sur Guy de Maupassant par François son valet de chambre, 1883–1893.* Paris: Plon, 1911. Despite Tassart's questionable objectivity, his work throws considerable light on the Maupassant who tried not to allow himself to be seen.
———. *Nouveaux souvenirs intimes.* Paris: Nizet, 1962. A less interesting continuation of the above.

VIAL, ANDRÉ. *Guy de Maupassant et l'art du roman.* Paris: Nizet, 1954. An exhaustive researching of the subject of Maupassant as a novelist. The lengthy analyses of the works provide little that the more brief studies do not contain.

2. Articles

GOURMONT, REMY DE. *Promenades littéraires.* Paris: Mercure de France, 1912. IV, 143–48. Very provocative.

HARRIS, FRANK. *Ma Vie et mes amours.* Paris: Gallimard, 1960, pp. 319–36. Interesting but suspect.

LEMAÎTRE, JULES. *Les contemporains.* I, V, VI (Paris: Lecène et Oudin, 1885, 1892, 1896), 285–310, 1–12, 351–59. Good, solid criticism.

NORMAND, JACQUES "Souvenirs sur Maupassant." *Figaro,* December 13, 1903. For all articles by Normand: interesting light on unlighted aspect of Maupassant's career.

————. "Maupassant et le théâtre." *Echo de Paris,* October 13, 1911.

————. "Maupassant et Musotte." *Revue de Paris,* November 1, 1911.

RÉGNIER, HENRI DE. "Guy de Maupassant." *Les Nouvelles* littéraires, April 29, 1933. An interesting, artistic article.

SARCEY, FRANÇOIS. "La loi sur les écrits pornographiques." *Le XIXe siècle,* July 4, 1882. For both articles by Sarcey: a contemporary attack on Maupassant.

————. "Bel-Ami." *Nouvelle Revue,* June 15, 1885.

SMITH, MAXWELL. "Maupassant as a Novelist." *Tennessee Studies in Literature,* Vol. I, 1956. An interesting evaluation of Maupassant's importance as a novelist.

SULLIVAN, EDWARD. "Portrait of the Artist: Maupassant and Notre Coeur." *The French Review,* December, 1948. Interesting discussion for readers with a limited knowledge of Maupassant's technique.

VIAL, ANDRÉ. "Le Mal de Maupassant." *Mercure de France,* April 1, 1948. Further clues regarding a puzzling problem.

WOLF, ALBERT. "Les Soirées de Médan." *Figaro,* April 19, 1880. More on the argument concerning what a writer should write.

Index

90169